DATE DUE

DEC 2 1 1994			
NOV 0 8 1996			
MAY 0 1 1997			
JAN 1 5 2008			
GAYLORD			PRINTED IN U.S.A.

*Composition as a
Cultural Practice*

COMPOSITION AS A CULTURAL PRACTICE

Alan W. France

Series in Language and Ideology
Edited by Donaldo Macedo

Bergin & Garvey
Westport, Connecticut • London

Library of Congress Cataloging-in-Publication Data

France, Alan W.
      Composition as a cultural practice / Alan W. France.
          p. cm.—(Series in language and ideology, ISSN 1069–6806)
      Includes bibliographical references and index.
      ISBN 0–89789–403–0
      1. English language—Composition and exercises—Study and
teaching. 2. English language—Rhetoric—Study and teaching.
3. Language and culture. I. Title. II. Series.
PE1404.F69   1994
808′.042—dc20   93–48970

British Library Cataloguing in Publication Data is available.

Library of Congress Catalog Card Number: 93–48970
ISBN: 0–89789–403–0
ISSN: 1069–6806

First published in 1994

Bergin & Garvey, 88 Post Road West, Westport, CT 06881
An imprint of Greenwood Publishing Group, Inc.

Printed in the United States of America

The paper used in this book complies with the
Permanent Paper Standard issued by the National
Information Standards Organization (Z39.48–1984).

10 9 8 7 6 5 4 3 2 1

Copyright Acknowledgments

Chapter 1 originally appeared in *College English* 55 (1993): 593–609. Chapter 3 originally
appeared in *Cultural Studies in the English Classroom*, ed. James Berlin and Michael J. Vivion
(Portsmouth, NH: Boyton/Cook, 1992), 296–311. An earlier version of Chapter 5 was published
in *The Writing Instructor* 9 (1990): 77–86. All are reprinted with publishers' permission.

To the memory of Jim Berlin

Contents

Foreword by Donaldo Macedo

As debates range among composition experts as to how to most effectively teach writing in a society where "[p]rint is not where it's happening," English departments, particularly in major urban areas, are fast becoming "literate" islands surrounded by a vast sea of illiteracy.

By illiteracy, I do not mean only the inability to read the word so as to arrive at some predefined meaning in the form of a competency-based skills banking approach. There is also a form of illiteracy, particularly political illiteracy, that is acquired through the university under the guise of professional specialization which prevents the development of the critical thinking that enables one to read the world critically and to understand the reasons and linkages behind the facts. The brilliance of Alan France's book, *Composition as a Cultural Practice*, is reflected in the clarity with which France provides a language of critique that deconstructs the instrumentalist approach to the teaching of writing and its linkages to cultural reproduction. The instrumentalist approach to literacy does not refer only to the goal of producing readers and writers who meet the basic requirements of contemporary society. It also includes the highest level of the "study of textual representation and signification [which] has increasingly become a means to erase 'the political economy of knowledge' and to 'reinstall the subjects in the discourses of dominant knowledges.'"

In *Composition as a Cultural Practice*, France succinctly demonstrates that even progressive composition experts such as Bartolomé and Petrosky who want to elevate students to a position of "textual critic," end up promoting a higher level of literacy as a form of textual specialization that functions to domesticate the consciousness via a constant disarticulation between the narrow reductionistic reading of the text and the "material realm" that generated the text in the first place. In reading *Composition as a Cultural Practice*, it becomes very clear that the inability to link the reading of the word with the world, if not combated, will furthter exacerbate already feeble democratic institutions and unjust, asymmetrical power relations that characterize the hypocritical nature of contemporary democracies.

France convincingly argues that a critical writing pedagogy must cease viewing "subjectivity and knowledge" as mere "idealized textual practices (signification, representation, interpretation)" divorced from the material context that forms, informs, and sustains these textual practices to begin with. However, it is precisely this form of anchoring "those rhetorical practices that privilege the critical experience of textuality" (the mechanics of signification) in the "material and historical situation of that experience" that even progressive composition experts such as Bartolomé and Petrosky often avoid—since it calls for a Marxist analysis.

One should not be overly surprised that progressive composition theorists in the United States such as Bartolomé and Petrosky would "waver somewhat in their commitment to a Marxist critique [by appearing] to avoid all but the most superficial definition of key terms of Marxist analysis." The unmentionable "M" word has such ideological power that it structures an academic reality that brooks no debate. That is to say, to be labeled a Marxist analyst provokes generally a negative effect that disqualifies all those who use Marxist critique as a form of counter-discourse to the present cultural hegemony. I am reminded of a well-known composition theorist who considers herself politically progressive and yet rejects any form of Marxist analysis.

When I was writing the book *Literacy: Reading the World and the Word*, which I co-authored with Paulo Freire, I asked her to read the manuscript. During a discussion we had of the book she asked me, a bit irritably, "Why do you and Paulo Freire insist on using this Marxist jargon? Many readers who may enjoy reading Paulo Freire may be put off by the jargon." I was first taken aback, but proceeded to calmly explain to her that the equation of Marxism with jargon did not fully capture the richness of Paulo's analysis. In fact, Paulo's language was the only means through which he could have done justice to the complexity of the various concepts dealing with oppression. For one thing, I reminded her, "Imagine that instead of writing the *Pedagogy of the Oppressed*, Paulo Freire would have written the *Pedagogy of the Disenfranchised*." The first title utilizes a discourse that names the oppressor while the latter fails to do so. If you have oppressed you must have oppressor. What would be the counterpart of disenfranchised? The *Pedagogy of the Disenfranchised* dislodges the agent of the action while leaving in doubt who bears the responsibility for such action. This leaves the ground wide open for blaming the victim of disenfranchisement for their own disenfranchisement. This example is a clear case in which the object of oppression can be also understood as the subject of oppression. Language such as this distorts reality. And yet, mainstream academics seldom object to these linguistic distortions that disfigure reality. I seldom hear academics on a crusade for "language clarity" equate mainstream terms such as disenfranchised or ethnic cleansing, for example, to jargon status. On the one hand, they readily accept "ethnic cleansing," a euphemism for genocide, while, on the other hand, they will, with certain automatism, point to the jargon quality of terms such as oppression, subordination, praxis, among others. If we were to deconstruct the term "ethnic cleansing" we would not only see how it prevents us from becoming horrified by Serbian brutality and horrendous crimes against Bosnian Muslims, such as the killing of women, children, and the elderly. The mass killing of women, children, and the elderly and the raping of women and girls as young as five years old take on the positive attribute of "cleansing" which leads us to conjure a reality of "purification" of the ethnic "filth" ascribed to Bosnian Muslims, in particular, and to Muslims the world over, in general.

I also seldom heard any real protest from these same academics who want "language clarity" when, during the Gulf War, the horrific blood bath of the battlefield became a "theater of operation," and the violent killing of over one hundred thousand Iraqis, including innocent women, children, and the elderly by our "smart bombs" was sanitized into a technical military term, "collateral damage." I can go on and on giving such examples to point out how academics who argue for language clarity not only seldom object to language that obfuscates reality, but often use that same language as part of the general acceptance that the standard discourse is a given and should remain unproblematic. While these academics often acquiesce to the dominant standard discourse, they aggressively object to any discourse that fractures the dominant language, on the one hand, and on the other, makes the veiled reality bare so as to name it. Thus, a discourse that names it becomes, in their view, imprecise, unclear, and wholesale euphemisms such as disadvantaged, disenfranchised, educational mortality, theater of operation, collateral damage, and ethnic cleansing remain unchallenged since they are part of the dominant social construction of images that are treated as unproblematic and clear.

France passionately argues that the price to astutely avoid a counter-hegemonic discourse that points to "a stronger pedagogical commitment to cultural materialism" can lead to the fragmentation of knowledge via textual specialism that produces an intellectual mechanization that, in the end, serves the same function as the fragmentization of skills in the back-to-basics instrumental literacy for the poor. Thus, the inability to make linkages between bodies of knowledge and the social and political realities that generate them not only produces a disarticulation of this same knowledge by dislodging it from a critical and coherent comprehension of the world that informs and sustains it, but it anaesthetizes consciousness, without which one can never develop clarity of reality. As suggested by Frei Betto, clarity of reality requires that a person transcend "the perception of life as a pure biological process to arrive at a perception of life as a biographical, and collective process."[1] Betto views his concept as a "clothesline of information." In other words, "on the clothesline we may have a flux of information and yet remain unable to link one piece of information with another. A politicized person is one who can sort out the different and often fragmented pieces contained in the flux."[2] The apprehension of clarity of reality requires a high level of political clarity, which can be achieved by sifting through the flux of information and relating each piece so as to gain a global comprehension of the facts and their raison d'être. Lamentably, it is precisely the political clarity dimension that is willfully lacking in the field of composition theory in the United States.

In *Composition as a Cultural Practice*, Alan France not only provides us with a language of critique to deconstruct the dominant ideology that reproduces cultural hegemony. He also provides us with a language of possibility that points to our ability to make linkages and "to insist on the material context of all discourse—as a social praxis—and to avoid 'the erasure of the political economy of knowledge.' " France proposes a composition pedagogy that rejects the passive acquiescence to subjectivity and knowledge as merely "idealized textual practices divorced from the material context that generates and shapes them. His insistent call for a writing pedagogy that points to action reminds me of Paulo Freire's categorical rejection of the intellectual "inertia that has irremediably chained us." A counter-inertia pedagogy

convincingly demonstrates that a critical reading of the world is intimately related to a historical and cultural reading of the world. Such a reading allows us to make linkages, comparisons, arrive at conclusions, and speak in relation to the world both theoretically and practically. In so doing, human beings become truly capable of reading the world, and in turn, able to intervene in the world in such a way as to affect positive change. Never is it possible to have intervention without a full comprehension of the complex sets of circumstances that have shaped one's immediate context. Therefore the comprehension of the object that does not trigger change ends up being an obstacle in the process of intervention.

The reading of the world under a permanent process of intervention, a reading expressed in spoken words, sooner or later would require its complementation through writing so as to be read. It is for this reason that there cannot be reading of text without reading the world, without reading the context. A reading of the world that omits the reading of the text implies a rupture of the inherent cycle that involves thinking, action, language, and world.[3]

NOTES

1. Cited in Paulo Freire and Donaldo Macedo, *Literacy: Reading the Word and the World*. South Hadley, Mass.: Bergin and Garvey Publishers, 1987, p. 130.

2. Ibid.

3. Paulo Freire, Foreword in Donaldo Macedo, *Literacies of Power: What Americans Are Not Allowed to Know*. Boulder, Colo.: Westview Press, 1994, p. iii.

Introduction

This book is an extended argument for taking the cultural context of writing instruction seriously. Since much of the best recent work in ethnography (Geertz, Clifford, Marcus) reveals the persistently local nature of historically patterned human behavior, my use of the word in a global—actually a national—sense might seem somewhat antiquated. From the outset, then, I want to be clear that by "culture" I mean the *dominant* process of identity formation that is reproduced by American institutions (especially the schools and the popular media) and that provides the basis for generalizing about contemporary social life in this country. Culture is the abstraction that accounts for the fact most of us, composition teachers and students, know the two-word phrase that completes "Less Filling, . . . ," but few know the six-word complement of "Give thy thoughts no tongue."

Stanley Fish's instance of a student raising his hand to speak in class makes the same point. And it is a better example for my purposes because it introduces another word that appears frequently in the following pages: politics. Hand-raising, like almost everything else that happens in our classes, is a sign of power: the instructor's possession of it, and the student's lack of it. The politics of hand-raising is not apparent; getting "permission to speak" seems *natural*, an almost visceral reaction of deference to institutional authority. It is becoming increasingly clear that teaching composition, granting our students a highly circumscribed "permission to speak" in their texts, is an inherently political activity because both the grant and its circumscription reproduce and reinforce existing relationships of power.

The denial of political conflict is deeply ingrained in American culture. We prefer to interpret our history as a story of establishing equilibrium, of solving problems, of working out a consensus—not *as* politics but *against* politics. When serious dissent rears its head in our field (as in the contention over English 306 at the University of Texas), when some group or faction refuses to bend to what dominant interests represent as the common good, it is characterized as "politicizing" the dispute.

To return to the popular media, the historical situation of teaching composition at the end of the twentieth century is, it might be said, up against the mall. A recent "television magazine" story illustrates my point. The journalist interviewed a retired couple who spent much of their time at a local shopping mall, videotaping the flux of shoppers. They often invited friends over to watch these texts of public life set against a backdrop of familiar brand names and retail outlets. "This is the new village green," the man told the reporter. "This is where everything important happens." For those of us in higher education, it is an ominous message for two reasons. First, the displacement of writing by images makes teaching literacy, and all the attendant intellectual disciplines, increasingly difficult. Print is not where it's happening.

A second and more complex problem is the displacement of public discourse by the languages of commodity production and consumption. There is no place for the "heated discussion" of the Burkean parlor in this new climate-controlled, hermetically sealed village green. The model of behavior is passive consumption of the familiar, an off-the-rack selection of a political position or candidate. Democracy has come more and more to mean not a political process of self-governance but economic access to the cornucopia of commodities on display at malls everywhere. As Stuart Ewen puts it, "The extensive choice and variety of images, which enshrine the goods we may purchase, is regularly [but deceptively] equated with a choice and variety in ideas and perspectives that we may hold or give voice to" (112). For those who teach rhetoric, this reduction of public discourse to a matter of style (the photo opportunity and sound bite) is a serious and immediate crisis.

Because the following chapters are avowedly political, I am responsible for as clear an accounting of my own agenda as possible. To do this, let me suggest an analogy between composition as a field of study and the "discipline" of economics. A recent essay on the taxonomy of economics identifies the three dominant discourses, or "schools," each rooted in what

Amariglio et al. call "entry points" or basic metadiscursive truths. By entry point, the authors understand

the concept or concepts a theorist uses to enter into, to begin, discourse about some object of analysis. . . . [It] can be, but need not be, an "essence"—the primary "truth" and/or the primary determinant cause—in the discourse that results. What all entry points do have in common, nevertheless, is that they are the primary concepts through which a particular analysis of some social activity is undertaken. (121–22)

Amariglio et al. identify three basic entry points for the study of economics: neoclassical, Keynesian, and Marxist. In the United States, neoclassical economics is the dominant discourse. It begins with "human nature," by which is meant rational self-interest, the "natural" desire to maximize ownership and consumption of resources in a physical world of scarcity. In the neoclassical discourse, "how individual preferences arise . . . is not properly an economic question" (128).

Keynesianism, while preserving a central role for the individual, shifted the entry point of economic theory from rational self-interest to essentialist structures of mass psychology and social institutions, which became the "real" determinants of economic behavior. Many Marxists carry structuralism still further, making "social class" the essential entry point. The discussion of economics in structuralist-Marxist terms begins with "the production, appropriation, and distribution of surplus labor" (136).

Amariglio et al. identify themselves with a fourth position, one they call "nonessentialist Marxism." Nonessentialist Marxism "refuses to recognize a center for economic discourse, [and] it asserts instead the proliferation and continued controversy between all . . . schools" (137). The methodological and epistemic key to avoiding essentialist entry points is the commitment to dialectics: there is no cause, per se, only contradictions and contention. As Amariglio et al. write, "Dialectics implies for us the idea that all entities enter into the constitution of all other entities and, therefore, exist as simultaneously constituent causes and effects" (136). Volosinov puts the point most simply: "Any real utterance, in one way or another or to one degree or another, makes a statement of agreement with or negation of something" (80). It is the operation of dialectical exchange that makes composition, in my view, the "cultural practice" of my title.

The affinity between the dominant discourses of economics and those of rhetoric and composition studies may already have suggested itself. To use Berlin's taxonomy, we might equate expressivist rhetoric with neoclassical economic theory. Both self-expression and economic self-interest are "entry points" for a humanistic discourse that reduces historical and social forces to matters of individual preference. And to stretch the analogy a bit, cognitivist rhetoric (in its more recent rhetorical or "contextual" garb) shares some similarities with the Keynesian view that "mass psychology" conditions—"mediates," to use Linda Flowers' formulation—individual rationality. For the cognitivists, of course, the psychology is not "mass" (i.e., social) but an inherent property of individual minds. Keynesian, too, are some variants of social-epistemic rhetoric that posit institutionally determined conventions of discourse as primary structures of the composing process. Keynes believed "that conventional and institutionally determined rules of behavior are the prime determinants even of so-called rational economic behavior" (Amariglio et al., 131).

The nine chapters that follow attempt, from different directions, to present a critique of these dominant theoretical and pedagogical discourses of composition and to propose alternatives. In Chapter 1, I attempt to historicize the contemporary practice of introductory writing instruction, especially the dominant discourse of self-expressivism, arguing that it functions to "assign places" to students in two ways. To enter this discourse, students must construct both a private "composing self," the authentic author of personal-experience narratives, and a public persona capable of performing the discursive work of institutional authorities. The result is a divorce of knowledge and power, which serves the needs of corporate employers but stifles the critical competence necessary for democratic self-governance.

Chapter 2, "Toward a Materialist Rhetoric," attempts to generalize an alternative to dominant expressivist conceptions of rhetoric. In it, I define and advocate a dialectical approach to reading and writing (a "materialist rhetoric") that teaches students how to reverse the distribution of power inscribed in texts by reinterpreting them from the subject positions of those "others" excluded from power by the reigning discursive authority. Consensual or pragmatic rhetorics, by contrast, seek conformity to conventions, which (I argue) are really textual inscriptions of asymmetrical social relationships—most often of race, class, and gender. After developing the argument for a differential rhetoric and giving an example of its pedagogical application, I conclude with a critique of (neo)pragmatism, the theoretical substructure of consensual rhetorics.

The next three chapters take up specific pedagogical problems associated with introducing cultural criticism into the composition classroom. In Chapter 3, "Composing a Post-Sexist Rhetoric," I explore what it might mean to take feminism seriously in the introductory writing course. The chapter focuses specifically on reading the rhetoric of asymmetrical gender relations in the popular media out of which students construct, in part, their personal narratives of identity. I discuss a semester-long sequence of writing assignments intended to lead students toward critical reinterpretation of cultural media (film, television, print images of advertising) that reproduce what we perceive as the "naturalness" of sex-role stereotypes. The chapter concludes with a discussion of the dialectical tension between what students actually discover in their research and what their ideology determines they will conclude about it.

In Chapter 4, "Radical Pedagogy and Student Resistance," Karen Fitts and I attempt a rhetorical analysis of student response to the encounter with teachers committed to social change—in this case, to a feminist critique of popular media. Against conservatives like Maxine Hairston, we argue that teachers of rhetoric cannot "impose" viewpoints on their students and that, indeed, American political culture imbues students with a number of rhetorical strategies that allow them to evade most of the consequences of any politically engaged pedagogy. We discuss five of these strategies that ideologically inoculate students against social change.

Chapter 5 makes a case for teaching vocationally oriented writing courses dialectically. After a brief theoretical rationale for a critical approach to technical and professional writing instruction, I describe my attempts to offer an ethnographic pedagogy whereby students take to the field to investigate not merely the pragmatic occasions of, but also the social and material conflicts inscribed in, institutional writing.

Turning to the recent history of composition as a theoretical field of practice, Chapter 6 examines the development of "cognitivism" as a discourse in rhetoric and composition studies. In building a theory of the "composing process" as a set of autonomous mental operations occurring outside of history, cognitivism insulated writing from cultural subjectivity. I argue that cognitivist discourse is itself an ideological response to the inherently political act of teaching rhetoric and writing and that, in the American tradition of pragmatic individualism, it provided the conceptual mechanism for preempting debate about social inequities.

Chapter 7 treats the politics of epistemic discourse theory, specifically the social-constructionist "paradigm" that appears currently to be the dominant theoretical formulation of composition studies. After examining the debate over the role of ideology in constructing discourse conventions, I conclude that a "particularistic" theory of the writing process (one that authorizes the uncritical advancement of local interests) threatens to deny our students rhetorical strategies for resistance and dissent.

Turning from theory to practice, Chapter 8 presents a "Chronicle of an Introductory Academic Writing Course." In it, I give a close-up account of my own attempts to use a social-epistemic or "constructivist" approach to knowledge as the basis for cultural critique. Beyond illustrating the day-to-day struggle to realize critical theory in pedagogical practice, this case study demonstrates one rhetorical stance (in my view, the proper one) with which we can prepare students to defend and perhaps even extend democracy in the increasingly "performative" world (Lyotard) of technological knowledge empires.

Finally, in Chapter 9, I indulge in speculations about the historically embedded and largely unconscious cultural presuppositions about the self and other that condition and constrain all discourses. These presuppositions can best be understood as "theologies," I argue. The dominant "theology" in the United States mandates the "owners" of discourse to divide the world into a self/other binary, precluding the community (the communion) necessary to genuine dialogue between dominant and marginalized.

At present, the need for reenvisioning composition dialectically as a cultural practice is particularly acute. While the project suggested by the present work is inspired by forebears on the left (Ohmann, Berlin, and Bizzell, to name three), I appeal specifically to principled traditionalists across the political spectrum, to whom the current rage to foreclose debate about our students' collective future, because it is, of all things, *political*, must seem nearly as odious and unscrupulous as it does to me. I have confidence, therefore, that those genuinely concerned with teaching the venerable practice of rhetoric as the basis for a liberating and humane education will not dismiss the central argument of these chapters merely because they appear to be "politically correct."

Chapter 1

Assigning Places: The Function of Introductory Composition as a Cultural Discourse

The introductory composition course is crucially implicated in the process of cultural reproduction. Its content is the set of discursive rules that assign students to their proper place in the institutional hierarchies of corporate capitalism (Ohmann, Berlin, Douglas, Susan Miller). When we teach students to construct an "authentic" self and to subordinate that self to the rules of a dominant discourse, we are reproducing ideological formations of truth, whether we intend to or not. In this context, writing assignments should be seen not only as work that the instructor is empowered to impose on students but also as a temporary grant of the instructor's power to "speak." The authorization to fill the "empty space" of the composition course with text comes to students from above, delegated through the instructor by successively higher institutional authorities. And students' exercise of this grant of authority confirms their "proper" place in the social distribution of power.

The argument advanced here asks for a broadening of the range of rhetorical positions to which writing students are presently assigned. At present, I believe, the range extends from a dominant self-expressivism to variants of social constructionism based on poststructural theories of reading and text. Excluded from the ensemble of assigned rhetorical positions is one that might be called cultural materialism, following Raymond Williams (210; see Brantlinger, 16–17) or, more recklessly, neo-Marxism. This chapter attempts to reenvision from the left existing practices of composition, which function to prepare students for their lives as producers and consumers of commodities, in order to clear the ground for a third rhetorical position from which writing might become an active means to transform the existing social inequities of commodity capitalism.

The argument will begin by establishing that the dominant expressivist practice of introductory college writing instruction serves to reproduce a kind of self-reflexive conformity at odds with the traditional ideals of a liberal education—but appropriate to the (short-term) interests of consumer capitalism: the training of a relatively privileged, literate, but politically quiescent managerial class who define success and well-being in the private terms of commodity satisfactions. Expressivist composition pedagogy assigns students places in this hierarchy by encouraging them to construct a private identity (a "composing self"), to authenticate that identity with narratives of personal experience, and to "mask" it from the impersonality of institutional demands of work.

In order both to illustrate the discursive position assigned to students by expressivist pedagogies and to demonstrate the virtual consensus expressivism enjoyed in our field as recently as the mid-1980s, I want to discuss at some length William Coles and James Vopat's 1985 anthology of composition pedagogies, *What Makes Writing Good*.

The second part of my argument explores the changes that "post-expressivist" critical theories of textuality have effected in composition practices in the last decade. In the course of analyzing the discursive positions assigned students by David Bartholomae and Anthony Petrosky's *Ways of Reading*, I will argue that the introduction of "cultural theory," while offering students *possibilities* for a politically sophisticated rhetorical practice, in effect merely replaces the privatized composing self with a neutralized "reading self," a discursive position equally divorced from political praxis or, in terms of traditional rhetorical education, from democratic agency in the public forum.

My purpose is not to evalute either *What Makes Writing Good* (hereafter *WMWG*) or *Ways of Reading* (hereafter *WOR*) as a textbook but to use each as a convenient source of representative—and therefore generalizable—examples of pedagogies that construct the student as discursive subject (or "writer," in the familiar representation of the communication triangle). *WMWG* was chosen because it includes specific descriptions of and comments on pedagogy by a large number of well-known composition teacher-theorists. *WOR* was chosen because it is probably the most sophisticated, influential, and widely used textbook that has integrated literary and cultural theory into its composition pedagogy. The focus of this argument is not on writing pedagogy as the technical means of eliciting critical writing (in any case, an impossibly controvertible term); it seeks instead to extend criticism from the experiential to the material realm by extending the range of discursive entry points assigned to students.

As indicated earlier, this argument emanates from the left, in particular the neo-Marxist "cultural materialism" of Raymond Williams and the Birmingham Centre for Contemporary Cultural Studies (Brantlinger, 59–67). But it hopes to appeal to a wider concern to preserve and advance the traditional role of rhetoric in enabling participatory democracy. The substance of these commitments is well expressed by Henry Giroux when he writes that educators (and, I would add, teachers of rhetoric and writing in particular)

need to develop a critical pedagogy in which the knowledge, habits, and skills of critical citizenship, not simply good citizenship, are taught and practiced. This means providing students with the opportunity to develop the critical capacity to challenge and transform existing social and political forms, rather than simply adapt to them. (74)

Since our students are subjects of a "mass youth culture" (Moffatt, 52–53), in which the self is fashioned out of electronically reproduced images of commodity consumption, the expressivist composing process reinforces the private enjoyment of status and material gratification as the primary values of life. By the same process of rhetorical privatization, the public discourses necessary to democratic self-government atrophy. In place of practice for civic life in a democracy, students learn a "supply side" conformity to the status quo, which is often represented in composition studies as stimulating the conventions of institutional discourses. Literacy is thereby reduced to a skill that can be sold to corporate employers to pay for a commodified "lifestyle" (see Rowe for an excellent discussion of this point).

To begin, let me set out in some detail the discursive practice that we have come to call expressivism as it manifests itself in Coles and Vopat's collection of writing assignments and related examples and commentary. WMWG supplies copious examples of the places assigned to students entering the discourse of composition and, in fact, offers a fascinating contemporary insight into the dominant pedagogical conduct of writing classes. In assembling their collection of pedagogical practices, Coles and Vopat solicited assignments, exemplary student performances of those assignments, and commentary on both from forty-eight luminaries in rhetoric and composition, representing the entire theoretical and political spectrum. Analysis of these contributions reveals the real content of writing courses as they were taught in American colleges and universities in the mid-1980s: a discourse assigning students to compose "selves" (Faigley, 408), to conform to the demands of institutional authority, but seldom to take critical—politically informed—positions toward the material culture that their texts serve to reproduce.

It is the flight from politics—the privatization of rhetoric—that I find most distressing in the discursive practices of composition studies in general and of *WMWG* in particular. Conceived of as a composition textbook, the collection claims to have "no party line . . . for a teacher to . . . feed to students" (xii). As the various chapters unfold, however, a "party line," intentional or not, does emerge. The platform is individualistic and uncritical, reducing the cultural context of writing to a repertoire of "roles," or masks, placed at the disposal of autonomous selves. This practice teaches students to subordinate themselves to institutional authority while preserving the appearance of individual freedom. That is, it serves the ideological vindication of extreme disparities of social power by constructing an interior "reality" where all individuals are experientially, if not materially, equal. Occluded in this discourse is the public dimension of rhetoric, which constitutes whatever ethical community might exist in a democratic-capitalist polity.

The rhetorical device by which contributors to *WMWG* center discourse on the individual is the metonymy of "voice." In the second chapter, "Moving Beyond Limits," for example, assignments by Robert Holland, William Irmscher, Janet Kotler, Susan Miller, and James Sledd point students, respectively, toward

1. a moment from your own experience or from that of someone you know in which a presumed [psychological] limit was found not to exist
2. an important choice about your way of life
3. [an exploration of what] separates a child from an adult
4. stories from each person that represent an important part of the person's life . . . in a public forum suitable for the class to read
5. brief imagined conversations [that] . . . give a different answer to the question "Who are you?"

Unsurprisingly, these assignments elicited self-referential accounts of personal experiences from students. The teacher/commentators' analyses imply agreement about what makes writing good: voice.

A clearly distinguishable "voice" defines itself in contrast to the external world of the writer's "experience." Holland comments on his student's account of overcoming a psychological barrier in gymnastics: "Her paper excels because she has been able to see her experience as a complex function of languages, ... both her own and her coach's" (15). Irmscher's student manages to "express a simple honesty that is quite beyond the capacity of more experienced writers" (18). Kotler praises her student's work as "first, an honest paper," distinguishing the writer from another student "whose own voice he has stifled in the name of Not Making Waves" (24–26). Miller commends "the controlled and contextualized honesty that good writing always displays" and the ability to use "an authentic voice in expressing your own experience and ideas" (31–32).

The quality of honesty that these teachers of composition find uniformly praiseworthy seems to be related to the students' ability to encode their texts in a personal voice. In the examples of student prose, the "composing self" is accomplished rhetorically by establishing a dialectic between an impersonal and threatening world and the writer's sense of alienation from it. Holland's student, for example, comes to terms with her "fear complex" as a barrier to leaping a vaulting horse, and Miller's, a motorcycle patrolman, narrates an incident in which he lost his leg in a hit-and-run accident. Kotler's student struggles with a learning disability and history of conflict in his family and at school. Irmscher's model student essay confronts the most impersonal and threatening adversary of all, "DEATH." Good writing, throughout the Coles and Vopat text, appears to be an existential (and largely ahistorical) struggle between the self and an unfriendly universe blind to human agency and deaf to rhetoric.

The implicit futility of public discourse is a leitmotif of most contributions to *WMWG*. Student exemplars record a process of personal adjustment to the world, acceptance—however reluctant or qualified—of the way things are. However, in Chapter 4 (appropriately entitled "Coming to Terms") the conservative political consequences of self-reflexive alienation manifest themselves overtly in an assignment by James Britton and Steve Seaton. It asks students to "write about any aspect of family relationships that concerns you at this time." In the model response, a young woman (Maggie) reflects on her experience of bringing a friend, Stuart, home to meet her parents. Stuart is something of a radical, "very outspoken, offensive even," and he "challenges" Maggie's parents about sending her sister to a private school. The parents "represent everything that is ordinary about life." Maggie "wants to be different from them," although she thinks she will "probably grow out of it." She claims to attend political demonstrations and to believe strongly in the causes they represent, but admits that "it's a way of showing my parents that I can look after myself. I like the feeling that I have a voice of my own, and that hundreds

of people share my opinions" (77). Maggie explains her political stance
in these words:

I've always been slightly suspicious of people who are completely, lock, stock
and barrel, radically left-wing. I don't think they ever consider their ideas and
their implications properly. I think it's better to have separate ideas about various
aspects of politics, and to have really thought about them, rather than to go head
over heels in favour of one concept. (78)

Although Maggie admires Stuart's courage, she "can never really break
away from my comfortable, safe, boring family," and will outgrow her
political ideals, marry, and have a family. She concludes: "We've got the
right ideas but we haven't got the willpower. It's not important enough.
Perhaps my kids'll be different. I hope so. Because I just don't care" (78).
    In Britton and Seaton's view, "a principle virtue of Maggie's writing is
in its *honesty*; one reads it with a continuing sense of the writer's struggle
to say what she means and mean what she says" (79). But what, in this
context, does "honesty" mean? "Coming to Terms" means, at least for the
relatively privileged like Maggie, embracing a "comfortable, safe, boring"
status quo (however reluctantly) in return for giving up "right ideas" that
are too much trouble to bother with. According to Britton and Seaton,
Maggie's "own life has indeed become observable, and the observation
achieves something—a gain in self-understanding" (79). Understanding
oneself ("coming to terms" here seems an appropriately commercial and
calculating metaphor) appears to mean embracing class interest; and
"honesty" seems no more than political expediency parading as disin-
genuous reflection. Self-understanding comes at the price of public discourse and political engagement. It leaves Maggie only a private "voice"
in which to comprehend her life solely in terms of her private interests;
the ethics of public life (the "right ideas") are left to others.
    The estrangement of private self and public world becomes a specific
step in the composing process as Chapter 7, "Masks," presents it. The
chapter begins with an extended quotation from Richard Lanham's
Literacy and the Survival of Humanism:

We may think of the self as both a dynamic and a static entity. It is static when
we think of ourselves as having central, fixed selves independent of our surroundings, an "I" we can remove from society without damage, a central self inside our
head. But it becomes dynamic when we think of ourselves as actors playing social
roles, a series of roles which vary with the social situation in which we find
ourselves. Such a social self amounts to the sum of all the public roles we play.

Our complex identity comes from the constant interplay of these two kinds of self. (185)

Like most of the contributors of the Coles and Vopat anthology, Lanham in this theatrical metaphor figures the self as a stable presence donning a succession of masks in the drama of social life. The self-reflexive, unified ego is the primary reality. It can be popped in and out of "society" like a program diskette. As "central, fixed selves," we must outwardly conform to those social roles "in which we find ourselves."

The central place of the composing process in inculcating the divorce of (self)knowledge and (social) power is suggested by Linda Robertson's contribution to the "Masks" chapter. Her student's essay offers a meditation on the tree and its unconscious participation in nature. In Robertson's words, the student "became what Donald Murray calls 'a magnet' for his subject. He drew himself toward himself; he became composed. Or to say it another way, his composing became a way of his composing himself" (196). Walker Gibson's selection, beginning with "the question of whether your experience of college so far has been one of 'freedom' or of 'regimentation,'" also idealizes the apolitical. The student exemplar of good writing is a stream-of-consciousness flow of intertextual debris from contemporary college life that captures, according to Gibson's commentary, "the pressures and absurdities of his immediate life." The "voice" avoids sentimentality and "politically . . . remains unaffiliated" (186–89). Again, the student is applauded for inscribing the divorce of self ("freedom") and social engagement ("regimentation") and, of course, for doing nothing about it. Authenticity is the positive measure of the self's alienation from its public identity.

The material conditions under which individuals must negotiate the terms of membership in their society are fully revealed in Chapter 8, "Public Worlds." Traditionally, the word "public" has referred to the collective of people who, in a democracy, participate in their own governance. The "public," a civil constituency, transcends the private concerns of private citizens; and "the public interest" promotes ideals of service and obligation to others—values that sanction the subordination of one policy to another. Public discourse, then, has been the primary scene of rhetoric—the art and science of adjusting individual utterance to global ideals and interests. But in Chapter 8, the editors equate "writing for or in the public world" with writing "certain people must know how to do well in the course of conducting their professional lives." Thus, "public" forums are reduced to vocational scenes of "business writing, technical writing, science writing, professional writing, industrial communication, and so forth" (219). And rhetoric, which traditionally has measured the legitimacy of individual interests by reference to the public good, is reduced to the effective pursuit of private careerism.

The chapter's four assignments reinforce the primacy of private interests. Linda Flower's assignment, for example, charges her students to adopt the role of a professional consultant. She cautions them:

Problems arise because two important things are in conflict. Try to define the central issues here; it often takes detective work and hard thinking to discover and define the conflict at the heart of the real problem. (228)

The model response to this assignment makes it clear that "central issues" and "the conflict at the heart of the real problem" are to be construed only within the organization for which the student-consultant works: a hypothetical mental health-care facility experiencing increasing demands for counseling in the wake of a plant closing. As local clinic administrator, the student-consultant assesses the psychological impact of structural unemployment on the community and requests reallocation of funds to deal with the problem. When Flower mentions the student's awareness of "a special set of long-term plans" for "facing the cumulative effect of prolonged unemployment" (232), she clearly does not refer to any larger constituency or to any public interest in, for example, government intervention to provide jobs for the unemployed. That would be political action, and as such, Flower implies, it lies outside the student's role as a competent functionary of the health-care bureaucracy.

The other assignments in the "Public Worlds" chapter further delineate the successful employee's apolitical persona. Carolyn Miller's contribution, a job application letter and résumé, cautions the student to "Write as yourself . . . including only factual information and assuming only valid personal preferences and objectives," and to "explain specifically what you (as distinct from your competition) can do for the employer" (235). The student follows these instructions to "both *fit in* and *stand out*," as Miller puts it. The key lies in one's "voice." She comments:

The letter represents your voice speaking, and it can make you sound inept, uncertain, uninformed, self-centered, pushy, presumptuous, immature, and so on. Or it can make you sound, as Mr. McDonald's [the student's] voice does, businesslike, responsible, enthusiastic, thoughtful, and good-natured. (241)

The "voice" of the applicant, like the "mask" of a persona, shields the self—who may not be suitably businesslike, enthusiastic, or good-natured—and thereby enables it to conform to the authority of impersonal corporate hierarchies, paradoxically without abandoning its "authenticity" and autonomy. And Miller praises her student's ability to interpret his "education, his work experience, and his extracurricular activities from the employer's point of view. He has learned to speak with a public, professional voice" (243). While the "Public Worlds" contributors are most likely reporting work assigned and written in upper-level preprofessional courses rather than in introductory composition courses, the imperative of personal conformity to institutional authority fits all too well into *WMWG*'s ideological program.

The dominant ideology of expressivist writing instruction, as mirrored in *WMWG*, reinforces students' social alienation and insularity by encouraging them to identify good writing with the ideal of the autonomous self, the "authentic voice," ignoring the cultural and historical determinants of individual identity. And reducing the "public" to corporate bureaucracies or to marketplace transactions neglects rhetorical practices with which students might think and write about policy. "Public" comes to mean institutional employers; "policy," adroit conformity to hierarchial power. Personal success displaces civic virtue.

With a few exceptions, like John Gage's stubbornly classical model of composing, *WMWG* presents "composition" as a fully articulated discursive program, one that has assigned students to adopt "comfortable, safe, boring" positions of private advantage (Britton and Seaton) and to construct a persona, or "public, professional voice," that assumes "the employer's point of view" (Miller). These dual theoretical tendencies perform their ideological work by masking the contradiction between individual self-fashioning and the hegemonic power relations of capitalist social organization. Since 1985, however, poststructural theories of textuality and cultural subjectivity have begun to offer composition students new ways to understand and even to contest their own interpellation as subjects of commodity capitalism. Nothing has been more influential than Bartholomae and Petrosky's *Ways of Reading* in reconceiving the writing process as a critical dialogue with pre-texts rather than as an individual assertion of identity. Nevertheless, my consideration of *WOR*'s (re)assignment of students to critical discursive positions will focus on its pedagogy's failure to escape entirely the expressivist privatization of rhetoric. While *WOR* has extended the range of rhetorical options for student writers, I will argue that (with a noteworthy exception in the recently published third edition) it has maintained the experiential focus of writing by means of its central trope, "reading" culture. After examining the limitations of *WOR*'s poststructural rhetorical positioning, I want to outline briefly how it would look if students' rhetorical repertoires were extended to include a materialist critical practice.

The analysis of *WMWG* in the first half of this chapter argued that expressivism relegates students to the rhetorical position of passive subjects who can maintain the human core of individual identity but who are at the same time well prepared to serve as creatures of instrumental discourse: the word processors who do the discursive work assigned by academic, governmental, and corporate hierarchies. Increasingly, however, knowledge itself is impeded by regimented, top-down patterns of discursive authority, as in the old-style, programmatic operating manual specifying policy and procedures from headquarters (as described, for example, by Freed and Broadhead). Instead, in many sectors of the economy, the postindustrial product—the processes involved in research and design projects, market decisions, legal strategies, and the like—requires a discursive environment in which information circulates in multiple and decentralized channels of communication. Two studies that explicate such regimes are Michael Arlen's *Sixty Seconds* (exploring the production of the original "Reach Out and Touch Someone" ad campaign of the late 1970s) and Tracy Kidder's *Soul of a New Machine* (describing the crash development program to engineer a new personal computer). Such a complex representational economy might be conceived, in John Carlos Rowe's phrase, as a "writing class," which would include, in addition to production-line technical writers,

market analysts, advertisers, communications professionals, and a wide range of elected and appointed government officials charged with the adjudication of the boundaries between the economy and the civic domain, between production and social life in the most general sense. (69)

The command economy of hierarchical corporations cannot easily accomplish these kinds of knowledge-producing transactions (a factor to which we may well owe the end of the cold war). The subject as producer of texts is a better model for this postmodern worker than the individual as conduit of authorized knowledge. Preparing students to perform the multiple critical practices that produce *readings* is the pedagogical objective of Bartholomae and Petrosky's *Ways of Reading*, a rhetoric reader that introduces writing students to the major texts of contemporary literary and cultural criticism. This text (the second [1990] edition of which I will refer to here) seems in many respects to be the antithesis of *WMWG*.

Instead of positioning the student as a self-unified "voice," a speaker of dominant discourses, *WOR* teaches students that they are subjects of culture. Instead of learning only how to conform to the status quo, students learn the critical practices that underwrite resistance. Instead of treating texts as exemplary models of style, truth, or wisdom, students are encouraged to examine the essays skeptically, reading "against the grain," as *WOR* frequently admonishes. Instead of "finding information or locating an author's purpose or identifying main ideas," Bartholomae and Petrosky write in their introduction, students engage in "social interaction" with sophisticated, often demanding, theoretical texts (1–3). Instead of asking students to assimilate their interpretations to authorial intention (finding out what the author means), *WOR* offers a complex web of sequenced assignments that positions students as practitioners ("strong readers") of literary and cultural theory (9–11): for example, (post)structuralist (Barthes, Geertz); feminist (Rich, Kristeva); social constructionist (Fish, Kuhn); and cultural materialist (Berger, Mark Crispin Miller).

In addition to topical questions at the end of each reading, Bartholomae and Petrosky provide fourteen assignment "sequences," each asking the student to realize theory in critical practice. Sequence Seven, for example, includes four assignments casting students as critics of popular culture in response to essays by Mark Crispin Miller and Simon Frith. Like many of the assignments in *WOR*, the sequence emphasizes the place of culture in conditioning media productions and their reception by the individual. Thus, students are asked, following Frith's historicizing of rock music in "Rock and Sexuality," to study contemporary rock lyrics, attending to "the power of rock and roll to shape, construct, or organize experience" (724). Another assignment in the sequence asks students to abstract a definition of "culture" from their reading of Frith and Miller, in the process "writing a kind of beginner's guide to cultural criticism" (725). Even in an autobiographical assignment in Sequence Seven, students are instructed to contextualize their own identities to cultural formations: "[write] on your experience as a participant or consumer in some area of contemporary American culture, perhaps including ways you might be said to be a product of your culture" (725).

Foregrounding acculturation as a primary process of identity formation is, in my view, a progressive step toward situating writing pedagogy and rhetorical practice in the material world of power/knowledge relationships. It subverts both the expressivist positioning of writers as autonomous individuals *and* the identification of knowledge as the property of institutional discourses (with the consequent effacement of public life). After all of the intellectual substance and critical sophistication of *WOR* is conceded, however, there remain important respects in which its pedagogy leaves intact expressivism's autonomous subject and reaffirms its acquiescence in the extant distribution of power. The problem is that the position of textual critic, which *WOR* assigns students, is no more politically enabling than that of experiential soothsayer. Bartholomae and Petrosky offer students diverse ways of interpreting the world, but for those of us interested in creating the rhetorical conditions for a genuine democratic polity, the point—as Marx said—is to change the world.

The problem with making textual interpretation the model of rhetorical practice has been stated most forcefully in a critique of the "textual studies" curriculum installed at Syracuse University in the late 1980s. In the name of (post)structuralism, Mas'ud Zavarzadeh and Donald Morton argue, the study of textual representation and signification has increasingly become a means to erase "the political economy of knowledge" (23) and to "reinstall the subject in the discourses of dominant knowledges" (25). The result is that "students may learn about the codes through which reality is constructed, but they are not placed in an oppositional subject position through which they can interrogate that reality and consequently intervene in its reconstitution" (22)—or, for that matter, in its refinement.

Bartholomae and Petrosky's pedagogy often affirms the divorce of text and world, which reconstitutes the student-subject as arbiter not of personal experience (as does *WMWG*) but of theory. This theorizing of experience is figured throughout as "reading." Thus, for example, in their questions and assignments relating to Jean Franco's "Killing Priests, Nuns, Women, Children," Bartholomae and Petrosky are primarily concerned that students "read the distribution of spaces" (205; *Resources*, 28), the imaginary topography (heaven, convent, home, brothel) that is the textual device Franco uses to characterize what no longer exists in many Latin American countries: the relative immunity of women, children, and religious from "the overarmed military who have become instruments of the latest stage of capitalist development" (196).

We might speak here of cross-purposes. Franco seeks to explain "unequal forces [pitted] against one another"—the instruments of capitalist development against traditional institutions "of Church, community and family" (196). Her territorial imaginary is thus firmly rooted in historically material *causes. WOR* points students' attention to the experiential *effects* of Franco's text. In the apparatus following Franco's essay, Bartholomae and Petrosky ask students to construct their own, North American, imaginary, and "at some point . . . speculate on the interaction between the imaginary and the social or political in national life" (Assignment 1); "to investigate a local site . . . [in] an essay that presents your topography and examine how it might be read" (Assignment 2); to apply Franco's imaginary as a critical reading of a Carlos Fuentes short story and to Harriet

Jacobs's "Incidents in the Life of a Slave Girl" ("Making Connections," 204–05). Rhetorically, these assignments all place students passively, in the role of responsive readers of the assigned text. The instruction in Assignment 1 to "speculate" (at some point) is the solitary reference to the material, the single requirement that students perform the intellectual labor necessary to determine why there are bodies littering Franco's text: Garcia Marquez's "thread of blood," Alaide Foppa's "disappearance," the death of Rodolf Walsh's daughter and the *montoneros*. *WOR* thus implicitly shifts interpretive attention away from this material world of death squads and the U.S. military aid that had armed them, and toward Franco's textual scheme, her semiotic diagram of women's domiciliation by relationship to the phallus.

Bartholomae and Petrosky also focus students' attention on deciphering cultural codes in their discussion of Jacobs's "Incidents." The material world of slavery, it is suggested, can be isolated from, and read as, a production of signifying practices. In "Assignments for Writing," for example, students are instructed: "Write an essay in which you try to explain the codes that govern the relations between people in slave culture, at least as that culture is represented in *Incidents*." And the authors warn:

Remember that there are different ways of reading the codes that govern human relations. What Jacobs takes to be unnatural may well seem natural to Dr. Flint [her unrelenting owner-pursuer]. Jacobs could be said to be reading "against" what Flint, or the Slave Owner as a generic type, would understand as naturally there. (355)

The focus again is on Jacobs's *experience* of her status as female slave; in the same way, students are asked to attend to their experience of the text—as a rhetorical production—and to its consumption as an artifact (353–56). A materialist reading would of course insist on deciphering the function of the slave as both labor and commodity in a historically specific system of production, that is, the extraction of labor and the consumption of sexual pleasure from the body of the slave woman. These are the material referents of the text, and they can hardly be understood without recourse to Marxist critical vocabulary.

The point is not that *WOR*'s (post)structural critical approaches to texts are unedifying. It is, rather, that such criticism stops short of interrogating the material conditions that called the text into discursive existence in the first place. Cultural codes are abstract and, to use the terms of Saussurean structuralism, synchronic; the historical struggles of African-Americans and women against appropriation are corporeal and diachronic, not to mention immediately contemporary. Anita Hill's and Clarence Thomas's conflicting testimony at the latter's Senate confirmation hearing, for example, might be represented as "different ways of reading the codes that govern human behavior," or of understanding what "may well seem natural" to Justice Thomas. But at least as significant a rhetorical issue is the differential power relations—of gender and institutional status—that allegedly enabled Thomas "to claim the same rights and immunities of masculinity that white men have historically enjoyed, especially the right to maintain open season on black women" (Fraser, 608).

Zavarzadeh and Morton charge that (post)structuralist theory is, in applications like the "Textual Studies" program at Syracuse University and—I would argue—in dominant composition pedagogies, a means of acculturating the subject "as a unitary, rational individual willing to participate in the established systems of signification that legitimize the dominant power/knowledge structure and its underlying economic order" (12). This process of legitimization means imbuing students with those rhetorical practices that privilege the critical experience of textuality ("the mechanics of signification") over the material and historical situation of that experience ("the politics of the production and maintenance of sub-jectivities"), thus assimilating the humanist "self" to its institutional double, the managerial "executive" (23). Richard Johnson has identified this disjunction between "structuralist" and "culturalist" critiques as a basic theoretical and methodological division in cultural studies:

On the one side there are those who insist that "cultures" must be studied as a whole, and *in situ*, located, in their material context. Suspicious of abstractions and of "theory," their practical theory is in fact "culturalist" . . . .

On the other side, there are those who stress the relative independence or effective autonomy of subjective forms and means of signification. The practical theory here is usually structuralist, but in a form which privileges the discursive construction of situations and subjects. The preferred method is to treat the forms abstractly, sometimes quite formalistically, uncovering the mechanisms by which meaning is produced in language, narrative or other kinds of sign-system. If the first set of methods are usually derived from sociological, anthropological or social-historical roots, the second set owe most to literary criticism, and especially the traditions of literary modernism and linguistic formalism. (50)

It is probably inevitable that rhetoricians who practice in English departments would prefer the structuralist to the culturalist criticism. Nevertheless, to give students a full complement of rhetorical practices, we need to insist that subjectivity and knowledge are not merely idealized

as textual practices (signification, representation, interpretation, conversation, etc.); we need also to insist on the material context of all
discourse—as social praxis—and to avoid "the erasure of the political
economy of knowledge" (Zavarzaveh and Morton, 23).

If the second edition of *WOR* largely fails to extend rhetorical practices
from the textual to the material realm, the substantially revised third
edition (1993) has taken steps to remedy the omission. In the earlier edition
(1990), Bartholomae and Petrosky's sidestepping of Marxist criticism—
even when a reading they were discussing was hardly explicable without
it—was remarkable. In Sequence Seven, Assignment 1, for example, the
authors ask students to "try your hand at [Mark Crispin] Miller's kind of
criticism"—the kind Miller deploys in "Getting Dirty," a close reading of
a Shield soap advertisement that concludes the TV ad tells "more than we
might want to know about the souls of men and women under corporate
capitalism" (405). The assignment, however, tends to assimilate this
materialist critique of culture to a decontextualized discursive practice for
students to learn ("developing a close reading of a particular show or ad
currently on TV" [723]) without regard to the implied critique of capitalist
division of labor.

WOR's third edition takes a further step in the direction of cultural
materialism, particularly by including a chapter from Susan Willis's *A
Primer for Daily Life*, "Work(ing) Out." In their introduction to
"Work(ing) Out," Bartholomae and Petrosky call specific attention to
Willis's indictment of capitalism as the primary causal factor in the
commodification of the female body. And in the five "Assignments for
Writing" that follow, they urge students, however gently, toward a
Marxist critical analysis. Assignment 4 specifically asks students to
"explain Willis's argument about women and their bodies under
capitalism" (727).

In the instructors' manual, however, the authors waver somewhat in
their commitment to a Marxist critique. While referring parenthetically to
their use of Frederic Jameson in teaching this unit and while asserting, at
the same time, the importance "for students to see that Willis was *not*
another liberal but was in fact critiquing the liberal point of view, which
is the farthest to the left that most of our students can imagine," Bartholomae and Petrosky appear to avoid all but the most superficial definition of key terms of Marxist analysis (*Resources*, 122).

It should be clear that my argument endorses a stronger pedagogical
commitment to cultural materialism. Students might begin with further
readings from Willis's *Primer*, particularly Chapter 1 ("Unwrapping Use

Value"), which is an accessible introduction to the elements of Marxist criticism. Students might then be assigned to practice materialist re-interpretations of other readings like Jacobs's "Incidents" and (in the third edition) John Fisk's "Madonna" essay. Specifically, they might explore the relationship of social practices to the extraction of women's labor and to women's dependence on men. In order to try out possible configurations of ideology, students might play (with apologies to Peter Elbow) the "mystification game," in which they invent narratives that would have the effect, if believed, of obscuring gross inequities of wealth and power between classes of people. Country music themes provide a rich source of mystifications. The main point here is that students should learn to shift rhetorical practices so that they not only can write personal, self-reflective essays and adept critiques of a variety of cultural texts, but also can assume a position critical of their culture's fondest truths.

This is perhaps not so radical a departure from the purposes of *Ways of Reading*. Bartholomae and Petrosky *suggest* to the student that "you might be said to be a product of your culture" (725). They tell instructors that they want students "to step outside a text, in order to ask questions about where it might lead, what it leaves out, and whose interests it serves" (*Resources*, 4). They say, "There is nothing worse than a class where discussion is an end in itself . . . ," yet they continue, "the point of the conversation should be to bring forward a *textual* problem and to demon-strate how, with care, attention, rigor, and precision, a person might work on it" (*Resources*, 4). And the authors make it clear that the end of textual analysis and production is not action but *reading*. They explain the writing process in these terms: "Once you have constructed a reading, . . . you can step back, see what you have done, and go back to work on it. Through this activity—writing and rewriting—we have seen our students become strong, active, and critical readers" (*Resources*, 4–5). In the sense that the student's interpretive "work" never has material effects, however, it could be said about *WOR* (and poststructural textual criticism in general) that too often reading returns to reading without ever passing the forum.

Those who theorize and practice instruction in writing are becoming increasingly aware that they are engaged in the discursive reproduction of one "truth regime" or another. That is, the rhetorical position(s) students are assigned to occupy determine(s) their understanding of agency as well as the terms of their membership in social formations. As teachers of rhetoric, we need not fear that students will learn to "come to terms" with the existing distribution of power. What we can and should offer students is the means to engage in a genuinely critical praxis. This move is in the direction of "cultural studies," as James Berlin, John Schilb, John Trimbur, and others have argued. Peter F. Murphy has lamented "the overemphasis on theory to the almost total exclusion of practice" in most academic cultural studies programs in the following terms:

Cultural Studies can work to create a progressive, insurgent culture. The reason to bring together a communications department with a sociology department is not just to allow sociologists to examine popular culture but to teach them to make subversive videos. The reason to unite literary theorists with drama professors is not to make better theater critics but to make better (that is, politically progressive) theater. (38)

As teachers of introductory composition courses, we must of course give students the rhetorical means to achieve politically regressive as well as progressive aims. It's been my experience, however, that once a student understands the dialectics of argument, she or he has a hard time arguing in bad faith (i.e., for policies sustaining oppression, misery, hatred, etc.) *in public*. Bad faith is easier to maintain in theory than in praxis.

The best way, in my view, to extend students' critical and rhetorical practices to their own subjectivities and to the material forces that shape them is to overcome what Patricia Bizzell calls our "willed blindness to Marxist thought" (*Contending*, 53). This means transcending—but not abolishing—the aims of dominant rhetorical expressivism represented by *WMWG* and extending—but not eschewing—the critical textual practices exemplified by *Ways of Reading*. Texts or textual practices are never inherently political; they become so only in the ongoing struggle to reproduce or contest material power. Assigning students to do even Marxist readings of texts in private does not offer students the chance to take conscious part in their own history. This can be done only by making rhetoric into a social praxis, by assigning students to effective agency in the ongoing struggle of history.

Chapter 2

Toward a Materialist Rhetoric:
Rewriting Hegemonic Discourses

A visitor to Fort Worth, Texas, can visit an attraction called Log Cabin Village, which consists of seven antebellum structures maintained by the city's Park and Recreation Department. One of the structures is the Howard Cabin. The department's brochure has this to say about the Howard Cabin and the Brazos River plantation on which it was originally located: "This was cotton country and surely the cabin was familiar with the rhythm of the banjo player and the 'hallelujah' of the negro spiritual for it was built by Mr. Howard with the help of his slaves."

This text poses a number of questions about the relationship between writing and reality. One might ask, for example, about the production of the text: What was the rhetorical situation at the moment the text was produced? There is assumed to be a writer or writers working to promote the municipal interests of Fort Worth. To put it materially (which is, of course, the objective of this argument), the city has invested money in restoring rickety cabins, moving them to a public park, and marketing them as a "tourist attraction." The anonymous writer (who sat at one time in someone's introductory composition course, no doubt) was thus presented with a ready-made and material purpose: the construction of a historical artifact. To achieve this purpose, the writer had to evoke an audience (Ede and Lunsford) who might be persuaded to visit Log Cabin Village, "visit" signifying here spending money in Fort Worth.

The images conjured up suggest a version of Texas and national history that the writer evidently believed most likely to attract tourists to Fort Worth. In addition to questions of text production, we would want to consider how the Log Cabin Village brochure might be read. One might ask, for example, what repertoire of critical practices students ought to be able to perform.

First, I think we would want students to recognize the persistence of racial stereotypes—the rhythmical and soulful slave, for example. We also might like them to chuckle at the image of Mr. Howard, sweating over his ax and awl in the Texas heat while his slaves obligingly pitched in to help. Perhaps more sensitive readers might notice that the text subtly blames the social arrangements that it represents on geography: "This *was* cotton country," after all.

Ideally, students might even do something deconstructive—undo the text's gestures of cooperation—such as the homely personification "the cabin was familiar with the rhythm" not merely of musical instruments but of instruments like the whip used in the extraction of slave labor. Whatever interpretive techniques they learned to practice, I would want my students to have the rhetorical competence to perceive the underlying material relationships that the text, in its very gesture of disclosure, attempts to obscure. In short, I want my students to perform a politically sophisticated criticism of what are called hegemonic discourses.

Such a rhetorical practice might proceed along the lines marked out by contemporary schools of literary criticism. The text under analysis at the moment, for example, draws on the same rhetorical strategy, binarism, as a racist joke. It invites the (white) reader to assume a position of dominance granted by our culture's asymmetries of difference and to exult in the power to identify oneself in opposition to the subordinate subjects of the discourse (blacks). The exultation, in the case of a racist joke, takes the form of ridicule. Here, it takes the form of a sentimentalized, pseudo-historical hauteur.

As soon as this line of critique is taken up, however, it is snagged immediately on the ideology of pragmatism. What do we mean by treating an advertisement for a tourist attraction as if it were a work of social philosophy? The work must be judged by how well it attracts tourists (its intentional effect), not by how well it serves the political purposes of academic criticism. Truths themselves, as antifoundationalists argue, are beliefs that have "turned out to be conceptually congenial, imaginatively evocative, and highly serviceable" (Smith, 132). Truth, pragmatists believe, is the outcome of negotiation.

As Greg Myers has persuasively demonstrated, rhetoric is used in doing science, in hammering out the conflicts that are inherent in any system of negotiation about what counts as truth (*Writing Biology*, 4). The rhetorical practices required to do biology (or to do business, as illustrated by Freed and Broadhead's contrastive study of discursive practices in an accounting firm and a consulting firm) are pragmatic. They place a premium on getting *measurable* results: grants and publications for biologists; profits and promotions for businesspersons.

A pragmatic system is very much (and very unsurprisingly) like a free-market economy. Everybody competes to grab as big a piece of the action as possible—within the system. "Truths" or "investments" are the result of a distributive consensus. Those who know how to play by the rules (or how to play around them) get the biggest distributions, and the entire system is insulated from criticism because it produces the "best" results—according to the *measure* that the system is organized to produce. So learning and obeying the rules can be shown to be the "best" rhetorical practice.

Judged by pragmatic standards, then, the Log Cabin Village brochure might well be counted a success. If many tourists accepted the text's gambit, entering the discourse in the position marked "Mr. Howard," they might well have flocked to the park to actualize for themselves a proprietary role in the romance of antebellum bondage and frontier violence. ("The plantation," we are told, "was not immune to Indian raids.") Results, in the form of increased admission receipts, would then offer a pragmatic confirmation of rhetorical effectiveness.

Learning to read and write critically is not an obvious outcome of this kind of rhetorical performance, which values conformity to a ruling system of signification. A pragmatic (or "consensual") rhetoric accepts a text's authorized version of reality, of history, as the only operative standard of judgment. This pragmatism has permeated contemporary rhetorical theory and composition pedagogy, focusing attention on persuasive effect. Meanwhile, the writing process is divorced from material context, the cultural and historical forces that, in the first place, determine truth and reality as well as the means to signify them persuasively. The major schools of composition studies work together to create the writer, both as a creative individual and as an institutional "position" or job, and to define writing as learning a set of rules—a pragmatics—for constructing texts (like the Log Cabin Village brochure) blind to their own role in reproducing exploitative class, race, and gender relations.

Expressivism creates a discourse of self, in which the subject writes from a metaphysical position outside history and culture, as the privileged term of the communication process. Cognitivism deceptively models itself on science, especially structural (autonomous) linguistics and cognitive psychology, assuming a mantle of neutrality that raises knowledge above the social and political contention inherent in discourse. What Berlin has called "social-epistemic" rhetoric (and others, like Kenneth Bruffee, call social constructionism) often affirms the proposition that knowledge is the result of a consensus within the hierarchy of established power/knowledge "communities." Discourse communities, when purged of hierocratic and hegemonic relations, become theoretical modalities outside of culture and history. Social constructionism has thus—perhaps unwittingly—mandated individual conformity to institutional discourses, helping to preserve the existing asymmetrical distributions of power. The metaphoric "conversation," which establishes consensus, takes place in abstract communities, where persuasion and "good reasons" (Booth), not conflicting material interests, determine the nature of agreement—where Mr. Howard and his slaves work together harmoniously to build Mr. Howard's cabin.

Very generally, then, I want to use the term "pragmatic" to describe rhetorical practices that seek equilibrium either by (re)solving problems that are contested or that defer closure, and thereby sanction the status quo, or by stipulating a decontextualized private role (a "voice" or persona) for a writer to assume in relation to the outer world.

To underscore my opposition to the exclusive pragmatics of consensual rhetorics, I will adopt the label "materialist" to signify the kind of practice best suited to cultural criticism (cf. McGuire, 200–01). A materialist rhetoric announces, first of all, its kinship to cultural studies, specifically the British Marxist heritage of E. P. Thompson and Raymond Williams. A materialist rhetoric is thus concerned to uncover the discursive means by which dominant social groups confirm or "naturalize" their dominance and by which subordinate groups contest or delegitimize asymmetries of power. The influence of Marx means taking seriously the subject's relationship to the means of production as a primary differential of identity: the difference between being signified anonymous "field hands" and proprietor of the Howard plantation. A materialist rhetoric is written not from the standpoint of the privileged self or of the privileged objectives of powerful institutions, but from the bottom up, so to speak. It contests the distribution of power inscribed in a text from the subject positions of those (i.e., "slaves") excluded from power.

From feminism, a materialist rhetoric borrows its preoccupation with the ways gender confers or withholds power: it insists on knowing how culturally coded transcriptions of the physical (the body) reproduce patterns of dominance and subordination. It "reads" a place for the anonymous mother of "[t]he young son of the family, Billy Howard." And it asks what interest is advanced by the Howard "family" giving birth instead of the woman.

Finally, a materialist rhetoric shares a methodological (if not an ideological) commitment to poststructural literary criticism. It insists on the disruptive reading of texts, on prying into the inevitable semantic disjunction between the writer's attempt to realize and control meaning and inherent instability, the polyvocal nature of language itself. Difference insists that meaning is up for grabs, that it is a critical and rhetorical dialogue between the writer's text and the reader's response. Therefore, "the 'hallelujah' of the negro spiritual" praises Moses, not Pharoah.

But a materialist rhetoric is not *antifoundational*, at least in its assumption that the material interests advanced or consolidated by texts are "real." They are "literal" in a double sense: as written representations of power and as material artifacts of institutional exertions of power in the world. They are founded on what Michael Ryan calls "gestures of exclusion" (3) both in the text and in the world. A differential rhetoric attempts to reconstruct the discursive positions of those excluded from the conversations where consensus emerges—those not invited to meetings of the mind.

PRACTICING MATERIALIST RHETORIC

The practice of materialist rhetoric will have significant, even radical, implications for the teaching of writing. If, as I believe, composition instruction is always indoctrination in some discursive practice, it is imperative for us all to understand what doctrine(s) we are inculcating. Much of the present work has attempted a *refutatio* of contemporary composition teaching, which indoctrinates students in a highly self-referential phenomenology: they are asked to perceive the world of phenomena from the privacy of their consciousness. This pedagogy seldom represents the world as a construction of the texts students consume and (occasionally) produce, nor does it present history and culture as textual realms students inhabit with others. Reading and writing can therefore be considered as consensual acts by which students conform to the conventions of textual authorities.

Initiating students into a materialist rhetorical practice requires means of critiquing the phenomenological world of texts. This critique must begin in the material world of everyday relationships, where the very architecture of daily life is structured in order to conventionalize relationships of power. For introductory writing students, not yet familiar with the university, an ethnographic foray into the hallways of institutional authority is a good starting place for a material critique. I begin by asking students to describe the classroom we are occupying, looking in particular for signs of power: insignia.

Beyond the ubiquitous spatial arrangements of classrooms—desk with lectern located panoptically front and center, student seats facing the "head" of the class—there are usually more subtle signs of power. A classroom I taught in recently was particularly rich in these signs. It had once been connected by a hallway to a suite of offices, and the locked door bore two signs: "Keep Out" and "Authorized Personnel Only." An air conditioner in the window was marked "DO NOT TOUCH CONTROLS." There had been an attempt to "childproof" the classroom, which the young women and men eventually discovered in discussing their descriptions.

While the material artifacts of the classroom and their arrangement can be "read" as part of a system of power relations, the university campus provides a much more elaborated code of hierarchical authority. Students will easily perceive the contrast between the president's or provost's office and those of a dean or department chair in terms of insignia of power: aesthetics of the building in which they are located, the existence and size of outer offices, the number of secretaries and their dress and demeanor, the richness of furnishings and decor, the noise level, and so on.

Once students have practiced the rhetorical analysis of the material world they inhabit, it is time to move on to written texts. Although not as obviously, these texts will yield to an analysis of social power in the same way that the physical "text" of the classroom or the university has. One assignment I have used with relative success to teach students how to read the social sedimentations reproduced by texts begins by asking them to read a news article titled "Teacher Wins Big in No-Pass, No-Play Lawsuit" and to "summarize the important issues in a paragraph or two." The story, in slightly abridged form, unfolds as follows:

Teacher Sue Collins won a legal battle with the Waco [Texas] Independent School District over her refusal last year to give a passing grade to a star defensive end.

The controversy cost the powerhouse Waco football team a shot at the state 5-A title in 1987. Now it could cost the school district, the superintendent and the high school principal $77,000 in damages awarded Collins on Friday by a federal jury. . . .

Collins, a teacher at Waco High School for 10 years, is still fighting to get back her job as an 11th- and 12th-grade sociology teacher. School officials reassigned her to teaching ninth-grade physical science after she blew the whistle to the University Interscholastic League last November.

In the midst of the 1987 playoff season, the interscholastic league ruled that defensive star Trell Payne was ineligible to play because he had failed Collins' class. The Waco team forfeited six games, including a playoff victory. . . .

Collins said both the principal, Wilbur Luce, and Coach Johnny Tusa pressured her to pass Payne, whom she described as a capable student, when it became clear he was failing. She said they suggested she join in a "team effort" by using a method called "point borrowing." She could raise his score by 15 points for the grading period and then subtract it from the next once his performance had improved.

A Texas Education Agency spokeswoman said point borrowing is not an authorized practice.

Collins said she had never heard of the grading option and doubted it was legal, but went along with their suggestion the first grading period and passed him. When Payne failed the second six weeks, she said, she decided to go to the league. . . .

Collins contends she was transferred because she refused to change the player's grade.

[The School District's attorney, Peter] Rusek, however, said the district changed her teaching assignment because officials were "concerned for her safety if she stayed at the high school."

Collins said she never received any threats.

But Rusek, noting how important high school football is to Texans, said parents, football fans and others were upset at the premature end to a winning season.

"You have to understand what kind of disturbance that caused," Rusek said. "They were one or two games away from playing in the state finals."

As part of her classes, Collins has sent her sociology students into the community to do volunteer work with abused children, abandoned animals, the Red Cross and latchkey children. She did not lose any salary during the controversy.

"I didn't lose one penny, but I did lose my whole career," Collins said. "I really was stripped of everything."

The sociology department she helped build was one of the casualties. The school district discontinued sociology classes after she was transferred, she said. (Reprint Courtesy of the *Fort Worth Star-Telegram*.)

This is a text that presents minimal difficulty to American readers of English. Even our basic writing students can read it, in Robert Scholes's sense of knowing the necessary generic and cultural codes for interpretation (21): it is a newspaper article, generically, about high school, football, and courts of law, all of which are familiar features of the cultural world our beginning writers inhabit.

Of the several hundred papers I have collected from this exercise, almost all include some form of interpretation (in response to the prompt, "summarize the important issues"). Only a few *just* summarize. The presence of interpretive gestures in the students' papers was signaled by the word "important" in the assignment, which asked students to "discover" a hierarchy in the events reported in the "Teacher Wins Big" pre-text. Scholes calls this "thematizing," the movement from the level of narration "to a more general level of social types and ethical values" (29).

What is most striking about the initial interpretations of "Teacher Wins Big" is that they almost unanimously conceive of the conflict as a private or personal one between the teacher, Sue Collins, and her employers, the school authorities. In class discussions of this assignment, as in the papers themselves, the major issue in dispute was whether Collins "won big," as the headline suggests, or was "stripped of everything," as she herself claims in the next-to-last paragraph of the text. Many students believed the teacher had won a moral victory by "standing up for her principles." Others pointed out that Collins's career had been ruined by her stand. As one put it, "nobody else would hire her now because she's got the reputation of a troublemaker." The article confirmed for many students the general corruption of public officials, the "dirty politics" of school administration, but no one expressed any surprise. To begin with, though, none of my students perceived the ironic dissonance in the story. And no one expressed any surprise that politics is dirty and power corrupts those in authority. The only real issue is where the individual draws the line of personal involvement.

My students, like those whom Michael Moffatt studied at Rutgers (*Coming of Age in New Jersey*), assumed that to protect the integrity (the "honesty" and "authenticity") of their inner selves, they must construct a public persona to deal with what is euphemistically called the "real world" and what means in effect the hierarchically organized corporate bureaucracies, which dispense the "success in life" that most claim to seek. For better or worse (worse, most of my students thought), Sue Collins had torn off her mask, jeopardizing her chances to achieve vocational "success." Even the elimination of the sociology program was understood primarily in terms of a career setback. The censoring of the high school curriculum and the consequent erasure of social knowledge went unremarked: just pragmatics as usual, the "natural" outcome, the survival of the fittest.

Thus, the "social types and ethical values" to which my students "thematized" their interpretations almost completely excluded any sense of public responsibility. If one has ethical qualms about a social practice, it is solely a matter of private scruple. With this view, it is not surprising that none of my students found the exploitation of Trell Payne, the football player, important enough to mention. A football hero who can get away with not getting an education is one of the "social types," like bullying or dishonest officials and dedicated if fuzzy-minded sociology teachers, belonging to the cultural repertoire that enables interpretation.

My students brought the social practices and artifacts signified in the text into conformity with their culturally determined understanding of material reality. This kind of interpretive practice underscores the limits of pragmatic rhetorical practice, which precludes students from interrogating their own viewpoints, their personal experience, and their familiar social bromides. Genuinely critical interpretive strategies require a rhetoric that exposes the play of material interests at work in the texts they watch, hear, and read.

The question that faces composition studies in the 1990s is whether it is our responsibility to teach students how to move beyond the critical practices I have styled "pragmatic rhetorics." Literary studies are somewhat farther along in the realization that textuality is a cultural process situated in history. Robert Scholes puts the case in these terms:

The interpretation of any single literary text, if pushed seriously, will lead us not to some uniquely precious exegetical act but to cultural history itself, which is of course a major part of our educational responsibilities as teachers of literature. (35)

As I argued at some length in chapter 1, the self-referential expression of individual experience has too often been the "precious exegetical act" of composition studies. We, too, have the responsibility to initiate students into the ongoing production of texts by enabling them not only to perform literary exegesis and effective exposition but also to discern in texts—their own included—the material conditions of production, the historical role of a text in the cultural reproduction of (and resistance to) power.

To this end, the "Teacher Wins Big" text, lacking an obvious pre-interpreted authorial point of view, is a familiar cultural artifact that can be made to yield considerable insight into rhetorical practices. First of all, it provides a wide range of differential subject positions—and, consequently, material interests—from which students can learn to reinterpret the events reported and their significance. The dominant positions in the text are occupied by the school administrators and the teacher, who are "worth mentioning" by name. The football player, Trell Payne, is named but remains a silent object of the text. And at the bottom there are those who remain nameless: abused and latchkey children, for example (with whom Collins's erstwhile sociology classes did volunteer service). Thus, the material relations that the text reproduces are elaborately differentiated.

A rhetorical analysis of these differences might begin by overturning the authorized hierarchy of the text. How, it might be asked, would winning and losing be defined differently by those in subordinate subject positions? A differential rhetoric would reinscribe the failing football player and the latchkey children who are "written off" by the very system that writes them as marginalized objects of authorized discourse.

Reversing this authorized point of view is a difficult imaginative act for our students. We have all gotten used to accepting reportorial authority, particularly in television news coverage of political conflict: a group of anonymous "demonstrators" mills around or past the eye of the camera; the "correspondent," our voice, interviews first a "protester," then an official or a spokesperson, who has a name, a title, and all the rhetorical badges of incumbency. The various and conflicting material interests of those represented are woven into what Gaye Tuchman has called "the web of facticity" (332). Authority remains undisturbed, the conflict being safely contained by representation as two opposing positions. And by the convention of "objectivity," a difference with two opposing positions is considered undecidable.

Developing materialist critical practices requires overcoming the passivity induced by this relationship to conflict. A materialist rhetoric can help students discern the hierarchy of privilege, and consequently the inherent conflict, in hegemonic relationships like demonstrator/official, latchkey child/sociology student, and failing athlete/football fan.

To introduce students to the practice of decoding material interests registered in social texts, I begin with readings from Roland Barthes's *Mythologies*, usually "The World of Wrestling," anthologized in Bartholomae and Petrosky's *Ways of Reading*. "Wrestling," with its emphasis on audience reception and its topical accessibility, clarifies for students the reciprocity of textual and social worlds. After class discussion of "Wrestling," most students will understand the work of rituals (like Texas high school football) in reaffirming and "naturalizing" cultural values. It is then time to write. I ask students to explain, in a three-to-four-page essay, "whose material interests (money, power, prestige) does high school football serve in the textual world of 'Teacher Wins Big'?"

The more astute students seize immediately on the relations between high school football and meritocratic individualism. For most, of course, the only real issue is how closely "winning" results from individual merit in the "arena" of free and fair competition. In discussing their papers, students most frequently argue about how well high school football "symbolizes" the work world they anticipate entering; or, as I would put it, how much the ideology of athletic heroics, cheerleading, and school spirit falsifies consciousness of material inequities.

Predictably, the more liberal students believe that competitive sports as represented in "Teacher Wins Big" favor "winners"—those kids whose families are already on top. "The system is really unfair to minorities," one white male student wrote:

They are told all they have to do is play as hard as they can and they will get money and Z28s. But, most of them are like Trell Payne [the text doesn't identify Payne as a "minority"], they end up flunking out [of] school. They don't get anything, like in the story, but they blame it [flunking] on the teacher. . . . All the fans get to do is jump up and down, so they don't get anything material. The only people that benefit are the coaches and principals. The "rep" of the school leaders is the only material interests [*sic*] served.

However, the dominant view of this class was expressed by another student (an African-American male), whose argument assimilated the hegemonic operation of high school football to the reigning Chicago school, laissez-faire economies:

High school football helps the system by making it more competitive. If the people on the bottom didn't learn to compete they wouldn't have any way to better their material interests. By football making everybody more competitive, more gets produced in the economy. From the viewpoint of poor people, this [i.e., the argument that football increases the GNP] is in the material interests of well to do people. . . . Getting to say how good the system works is one of the things you compete for.

Like the two students quoted here, nearly everyone in the classes who wrote on this topic demonstrated some understanding that the written text was a representation of a social text (a patterned fabric of material interests) and that the "pattern," ritualized high school athletics, served the interests of some better than it did others.

In addition to the hierarchy of subject positions, we might ask as well about the hierarchy of values inscribed in the text. What kind of winning or losing counts most? What kind is unimportant or totally ignored? And who gets to decide which is which?

A materialist rhetoric attempts to reverse the authorized axiology of the text as well as its distribution of power. In "Teacher Wins Big," winning is the dominant value, and it is measured in dollars, points, titles, and grades. Winning is good for those at the top, not so good for those in depreciated positions in the text (and, inevitably, in the world). Winning is associated with power and violence. The aggression that is good for defensive football backs and for winning state championships (and thus for the school administration) is not so good for abused children or for the teacher (allegedly) threatened with physical harm for placing education over athletics. By contrast, "losing" in the text is mainly intangible: the education of the student athlete, the abolition of the sociology program, the neglect and abuse of children. A materialist rhetoric, therefore, will ask students to turn things upside down, reevaluating the text in the interest of the subordinate and nameless others.

College students, who are inclined to conform to the rules for winning and losing, do not take naturally to this kind of insubordination. They are inclined toward a rhetoric of consensus, which is concerned to establish an agreement about what a text means *to them*. They are, to use Richard Rorty's words, concerned about what best allows "us . . . to cope with various bits of the universe" ("Pragmatism," 61)—the particular bits that affect "us." The "us," of course, are the subjects authorized to speak the discourse, those not excluded by lack of cultural capital from the conversation.

When my students considered "Teacher Wins Big" collaboratively, in small discussion groups, they did reach a consensus: what was "important" was the impact of events on the career of the teacher. The story was a cautionary tale about an individual caught in the political machinations of the educational bureaucracy that employed her. This interpretation, which largely ignored the silenced subjects and values of the text, best allowed them to cope with their universe. It was pragmatic.

In order to draw students' attention to the "situatedness" of values—the fact that winning and losing are a matter of one's perspective—I asked my class to map out the conflicting interests recorded in "Teacher Wins Big." The resulting "Winners and Losers" diagram seemed to underscore for students the reality that dominant definitions of winning and losing reinforce the material interests of those occupying positions of power in the text's semiosis.

We began this project by identifying and arranging hierarchically the subject positions offered by the news story. The list of subjects occupied the left margin of the chart: (1) the school district's attorney, Rusek; (2) the principal, Luce; (3) Coach Tusa; (4) football fans; (5) Sue Collins; (6) sociology students; (7) Trell Payne; (8) abused and latchkey children.

Ranking these positions in terms of social power provided a lively discussion, especially the place marked "fans." Was this the vox populi? If so, it should be placed at the top of the hierarchy. Was it a gang of violent and ignorant hooligans? If so, it should be at the bottom, just ahead of "children." Several students argued for a connection between the violent threats against Sue Collins and the problem of child abuse in the community. Or, as some wondered, were the "football fans" (the ones who threatened Collins's safety) a figment of Mr. Rusek's imagination, a complete fabrication? In this case, "football fans" weren't really *subjects* at all. The outcome was a compromise that located the football fans in a medial position just above Sue Collins because, it was reasoned, they carried more weight with the school administration than did the former sociology teacher.

Next, along the top of the chart, students recorded the major events, the specific instances of winning and losing: (1) completion of winning season; (2) 5-A title forfeiture; (3) $77,000 award to Collins; (4) Trell Payne's failure in sociology ("loss of eligibility"); and (5) loss of the sociology program. Finally, students determined whether, from the viewpoint of each subject position, a particular event should count as winning (W), losing (L), or "makes no difference" (X).

In abbreviated form, the "Winners and Losers" chart looked like this:

Position	Winning Season	Loss of Title	$77,000 Award	Payne's Failure	End of Sociology
Attorney	X	X	L	X	X
Principal	W	L	L	L	X (or W)
Coach	W	L	L	L	X
Fans	W	L	X	L	X (or W)
Collins	X	X	W	X	L
Students	X	X	X	X	L
Trell Payne	W	L	X	L	X
Children	X	X	X	X	X (or L)

Although the chart's significance was variously interpreted, one point earned a consensus: the interests of the school administration were at odds not only with Collins's but also with those of the students and children inscribed in the text.

To read the full range of cultural practices in "Teacher Wins Big," students need to rewrite the authorized text from the subject positions of those excluded from power. A rhetoric of difference must reject the "conversation" trope because it implies a false textual egalitarianism that ignores the existence of failing athletes and latchkey children. Those having no "voice" can be written only by a nonconsensual discourse. The negation of the voiceless other is, however, the all too likely outcome of rhetorics of consensus that are rooted in self-reflexive concerns: the "us" coping with the universe.

The conversation metaphor suggests that knowledge and power are equally diffused—like linguistic competence—throughout a society, and that all members enjoy standing invitations to what Michael Oakeshott called the "conversation of mankind." The contention over the established distribution of power in any society is far more subtle than collaborative rhetorics would have it: "knowledgeable peers" reaching consensus in discourse communities. In fact, rhetorics of consensus themselves are instrumental in advancing and consolidating the established apportionment of power by directing attention away from real or potential conflict. They consolidate dominant discourses by withholding from dissent the sanction of "knowledge" and, of course, by ignoring the interests of those excluded from the conversation.

Of course, in terms of the global needs of writing instruction—that is, *in practice*—dividing rhetoric into two antagonistic domains, pragmatic and materialist, creates a false dichotomy. If students did not learn to conform to discursive conventions, they would not be able to read or write at all. And the interpretive act that "makes meaning" (that thematizes texts to cultural codes, in Scholes's terms) begins with a passive appropriation of those codes. Readers have to begin by agreeing on what signifiers like "slaves" and "latchkey children" mean. This is a pragmatic act of conformity to conventions.

Nevertheless, we should have much confidence in students' mimetic abilities to conform to the codes of dominant discourses, which have pleasures, prerogatives, and power to confer. What is largely missing from writing instruction is the rhetorical competence to resist textual authority, to read the repressed difference from the traces—or scars—left on the page. This is the rhetorical competence that will best prepare students for a cultural studies curriculum, which I hope is the direction that education will be taking as the millennium approaches.

PRAGMATISM AND THE POLICE

In his magnificent "genealogy" of American pragmatism, *The American Evasion of Philosophy*, Cornel West attempts to discern a distinctive, indigenous intellectual heritage that has sought more or less radically to promote an "Emersonian culture of creative democracy by means of critical intelligence and social action" (212). Thanks to his scholarly candor, however, West has, in the process of qualifying his claims, argued a more convincing case for the pragmatic tradition as elitist damage control than as inspiration for political and moral action. His Emerson "not only prefigures the dominant themes of American pragmatism but, more important, enacts an intellectual style of cultural criticism that permits and encourages American pragmatists to swerve from mainstream European philosophy" (9). Yet, he concedes, Emerson "celebrates moral transgression [the exercise of personal conscience against custom, law, and tradition] at the expense of social revolution" (17). Emerson's vision "highlights individual conscience along with political impotence, moral transgression devoid of fundamental social transformation, power without empowering the lower classes" (40).

West asserts that "American pragmatism reaches its highest level of sophisticated articulation and engaged elaboration in the works and life of John Dewey" (69). But like Emerson, Dewey distrusts "resolute ideological positioning, as in political parties and social movements from below . . . [and] he believes that social conflict can be resolved and societal problems overcome by a widely held consensus" (102). And of Richard Rorty, West writes that his

neopragmatic project for a postphilosophical culture is an ideological endeavor to promote the *basic* practices of liberal bourgeois capitalist societies . . . [and] a fervent vigilance to preserve the prevailing bourgeois way of life in North Atlantic societies, especially American society. (206)

These convictions are profoundly hostile to any serious reapportionment of social power. They betray instead a strategic means of vitiating serious criticism of privilege in American society. It is only by positing a "prophetic" strain in the pragmatic tradition that West can speak of "an Emersonian culture of creative democracy in which the plight of the wretched of the earth is alleviated" (235). He is certainly not referring to Rorty here; indeed, his book concludes with long quotations of Raymond Williams and Antonio Gramsci.

It is not surprising, then, to find that the dominant consensual theory of composition, social constructionism, is intimately related to the American pragmatic tradition. As I argued in the preceding chapter, Kenneth Bruffee must be credited with the social constructionist synthesis. His influential 1986 *College English* essay, "Social Construction, Language, and the Authority of Knowledge," is a veritable celebration of the "new pragmatism" (773), drawing more directly on the writings of Thomas Kuhn and Richard Rorty. Two years earlier, Bruffee had introduced the "conver-

sation" metonymy as part of his (likewise influential) argument for collaborative learning in the writing class. Through this figure, he appropriated the major rhetorical convention of pragmatist discourse: a
gathering of peers (as in "peer groups") ruled not by social or political
interests but by reason.

While he admits in his 1984 article that conversations may be constrained "by ethnocentrism, inexperience, personal anxiety, economic
interests, and paradigmatic inflexibility" (639), Bruffee easily envisions
discourse occurring in "a community of status equals: peers" (642). He
idealizes the "Conversation of Mankind" as an exchange taking place in
an ahistorical present, unconstrained by the hegemonic structuring of
discourses or by radically unequal access to forums. It is worth noting that
the "conversation" trope comes to Bruffee from Richard Rorty, who
adopted it from Michael Oakeshott's *The Voice of Poetry in the Conversation of Mankind.* Kenneth Burke's earlier but similar analogy does not
appear to be in Bruffee's mind, perhaps because for Burke it is a "heated
discussion" rooted in history.

Unlike Burke's metonymy, Oakeshott's appears to be located outside
social and historical exigencies in a kind of trans-Stygian ethereality:

> The participants are not engaged in an inquiry or a debate; there is no "truth" to
> be discovered, no proposition to be proved, no conclusion sought. They are not
> concerned to inform, to persuade, or to refute one another . . . ; they may differ
> without disagreeing. . . . Nobody asks where they have come from or on what
> authority they are present. . . . There is no symposiarch or arbiter; not even a
> doorkeeper to examine credentials. (10–11)

There is, in other words, no place for rhetoric or for the material interests
that rhetoric is concerned with advancing. This is consensual rhetoric with
a vengeance, a conversation that must be precisely what Bruffee had in
mind with his "communities of status equals."

But as Oakeshott reveals, the heterogeneous and egalitarian assemblage
that is implied by unrestricted entry rests on a common solidarity of social
interests. The participants in the "Conversation of Mankind" are "play
fellows moved . . . only by their loyalty and affection for one another"
(14). People do not come to make trouble, and women apparently don't
come at all, making the conversation literally one of "mankind."

There is, in any case, a "symposiarch" in attendance at meetings like
Oakeshott's, present in the very ideological formations (or "discourse
conventions") of linguistic currency. As we have seen, Freed and Broadhead demonstrated in their study of corporate discursive practices that the

hierarchical relationships at the Alpha and Omega companies depend on their codification in "sacred texts," or operating manuals. Once textualized, power relationships become legitimized as knowledge and can, in turn, wield power. Operating manuals—literal and figurative—function as symposiarchs at the "Conversation of Mankind."

And there is a doorkeeper as well, who, to continue Oakeshott's metaphor, denies admission to the lower orders. By social convention, the privileged "play fellows" alone are ushered in. The rabble would not know how to behave, much less speak, and there is always the danger that they might fall upon the claret and cigars. This doorkeeper is literacy.

Outside the rarefied world of Oakeshott's coterie, arguments break out, a possibility that he finds particularly lamentable. The "established monopoly" of critical discernment

will not only make it difficult for another voice to be heard, but it will also make it seem proper that it should not be heard: it is convicted in advance of irrelevance. And there is no easy escape from this *impasse*. An excluded voice may take wing against the wind, but it will do so at the risk of turning the conversation into a dispute. (15)

It is clear that a system of discourse like the "Conversation of Mankind" is inherently hierarchical. It denies a place to those who dissent and marginalizes the powerless about whom the discourse speaks. In this sense, it is part of what Giles Gunn calls the "imperialism of consciousness," which has been used to police outbreaks of radicalism since antiquity.

For Oakeshott, of course, the conversation is about poetry and the cultivation of aesthetic discernment and literary sensibility. While few today would insist that this is a politically innocent preoccupation, Rorty has appropriated the conversation trope to insulate the status quo from dispute. This is true explicitly, as when he writes, that "we should be more willing than we are to celebrate bourgeois capitalist society as the best polity actualized so far, while regretting that it is irrelevant to most of the problems of most of the population of the planet" (*Consequences*, xliii). And the implicit elitism of Oakeshott's conversation trope occasionally shows up in Rorty's text, for example, when he contrasts his clubby skepticism with "what the vulgar call 'truth'" ("Pragmatism," 29).

However, it is the consensual "we" that does the police work for pragmatism on Rorty's beat. This rhetorical move opens a privileged space in the pragmatic discourse, proffering an alliance between writer and reader. Reading as an act of consensus cements this alliance between status equals, at the same time closing off consideration of interests in conflict with those of the conversants. Here is John Dewey writing in *Individualism: Old and New* (1929):

To gain an integrated individuality, each of us needs to cultivate his own garden. . . . Our garden is the world, in the angle at which it touches our own manner of being. By accepting the corporate and industrial world in which we live, and by thus fulfilling the precondition for interaction with it, we, who are also parts of the moving present, create ourselves as we create an unknown future. (quoted in West, 103–04)

The consenting readers of this text are offered the mantle of philosophical interlocution. They become peers of the philosopher, capable of creating themselves by tilling their gardens. There is no entry point in this text for the factors of "the corporate and industrial world" or their much different interests. They remain the faceless workers, the others written by the discourse. On the other hand, "we" cultivate our own gardens; we create ourselves as we accept the system that marginalizes them. Rorty uses the same strategy: "we should be more willing than we are to celebrate bourgeois capitalist society" (*Consequences*, 210).

A consensual rhetoric authorizes to speak only those recipients of gilded, embossed invitations to the "Conversation of Mankind," to return to Oakeshott's trope. The invitations allow recipients to construct metaphysical—although frequently unnamed—positions outside of culture and history: the self, the named, the referent of "we." Those not invited to attend are the written objects of the privileged discourse.

A materialist rhetoric recognizes those occupying subject positions incorporated in texts and their material, as well as discursive, subordination to structures of power. It resists privileging an "outside" position from which an "invitee" to the conversation can ask, for example, "questions about what will help us get what we want (or about what we *should* want)" or what is or is not a "profitable topic" (Rorty, "Pragmatism," 61). What "we" want or should want or find profitable is always a matter of our relationship to power.

To paraphrase Gertrude Stein, there is no outside outside the social text: only by learning to compose that outside do the privileged, we and our students, write our own invitations to the conversation of mankind. And in the process of learning to do this, we exclude the silent and subordinate others in the interest of consolidating our own privileges. A materialist rhetoric, by contrast, teaches students to reverse, rhetorically at least, the system of privileges that puts them in control of the pen.

Chapter 3

Composing a Post-Sexist Rhetoric: Introductory Writing Instruction as a Cultural Production

Most institutions of higher learning have adopted some official policy to eliminate sexist language from discourses of knowledge and administration. Drawn from sources like "NCTE Guidelines for Nonsexist Language," such policy statements recognize, at least implicitly, the role of language in reproducing social realities. At the university where I teach, the president has circulated a pamphlet, *Guidelines for Avoiding Gender-Biased Language in University Communications*, for "the purpose of emphasizing the University's commitment to equal opportunity for all." In the introduction to this document, he "discourages any use of language that reinforces stereotypes or inappropriate attitudes concerning gender roles" and mandates that "[a]ll official University communications, either written or oral, shall be free of gender-biased language."

Those of us who take these aims seriously are perhaps entitled to skepticism about the depth of commitment to social change implied by calls for the elimination of sexist language. Nearly everything we know about the history of language, after all, suggests that changing social practices drive linguistic change, and not the other way around. Nevertheless, following Antonio Gramsci, we might consider the ideology of "equal opportunity" as one of those "concessionary" moments when "[w]hat was previously secondary and subordinate . . . becomes the nucleus of a new ideological and theoretical complex" (p. 195). For while it is easy to complain of institutional duplicity and cynicism, an official policy against sexism might well provide the nucleus for progressive curricular and even institutional change. Toward that end, I want to explore one way to help implement—or at least take advantage of—official initiatives against gender-biased language.

The representation of "stereotypes and inappropriate attitudes" in language perpetuates asymmetries of social power and opportunity. This much *Guidelines* explicitly concedes by linking its commitment to non-sexist language to its affirmative-action policy. If language represents inequities, then the necessary next step is to examine the cultural sources of gender-biased language: the material inequities signified in and re-produced by discourse. *Guidelines* proscribes the generic use of "man" and male pronouns, use of gender-coded occupational terms, and patronizing references to a stereotypical world of logical men and emotional women. It mandates parallel *language* for men and women. Yet everything we know about linguistic change suggests its dependence on social and material change. The word "sexism" describes a condition of social subordination, a material world where occupations *are* typically gender-coded and women (and men) *are* stereotyped.

To integrate university initiatives on nonsexist language into the curriculum, therefore, we must design courses that examine the cultural construction of gender inequities in the material and imaginary world our students actually inhabit. Such a program is primarily rhetorical because it involves, in Walter Beale's words, "the process by which social ideals and constructions of reality are given voice and emphasis in historical situations" (p. 633). Introductory college writing courses, where most students are initiated into rhetorical practices, seem the ideal place to incorporate fully the mandates of university policies into the curriculum. By teaching students how to investigate the rhetoric of gender representations in the media they consume, introductory composition instructors can deepen students' understanding of how culture attributes differential meaning to sexual identity.

Such a "post-sexist" rhetoric requires the exercise of moral authority and a political commitment to change. But even without serious institutional commitment to social change (which in any case seems utopian), liberal gestures can underwrite curricular reform. As Patricia Bizzell puts it, "An argument against sexism can make use of values concerning human equality and fair play that even some sexists may hold" ("Beyond Anti-Foundationalism," p. 672). The openings provided by university initiatives like affirmative action and nonsexist language (and a number of others under rubrics like critical thinking, ethical implications of knowledge, and ecological responsibility) can be cited to authorize the critical study of culture as the practice of rhetoric.

Institutional initiatives against gender-biased language seek to promulgate change by adding one more category of rules to the bulging current-traditional handbook. This emphasis on propriety obscures the relationship between language and society. To integrate proscriptions of gender-biased language into the curriculum, we will need to "teach the conflict" (in Gerald Graff's words) between egalitarian ideals and actual social practices. The introductory composition course is the ideal laboratory to examine the social practices that manifest themselves ultimately in linguistic differences of worth, power, and freedom. Before I get to a description of the composition course as laboratory for cultural studies, however, I must acknowledge the political realities that circumscribe writing instruction.

As the nationally orchestrated attack on Linda Brodkey's reform of the writing program at the University of Texas illustrates, a serious program of cultural studies—one that moves from platitudes to politics—can expect to encounter resistance in most academic settings. If the study of the rhetoric and reasoning of civil rights law can be characterized as "political indoctrination supplanting education" (George Will), institutionalizing the study of gender inequities must remain utopian.

But integrating cultural studies into introductory writing programs also violates dominant theoretical orientations of rhetoric and composition as a field of knowledge. As James Berlin has argued, self-expressivist and cognitivist rhetorics organize the writing process in specifically ideological ways: they focus attention on the writer as the maker of meaning and privileged interpreter of his or her own experience. In other words, they ignore the cultural subjectivity of individual meaning and experience. But because the writer is already a gendered subject, she or he cannot—without a critical (i.e., political) theory of cultural formation—get outside culturally ascribed identities of self and other. Annette Kuhn describes self-identity in our culture this way: "subjectivity is always gendered and every human being is, and remains, either male or female. . . . Moreover, in ideology gender identity is not merely absolute: it also lies at the very heart of human subjectivity" (p. 52). Asking the writer to reflect on her gender or to discover a solution to the "problem" of sexism will leave untouched the ways the writer herself is constituted as a subject of her own ideology.

If, however, institutional and ideological resistance to gender studies in the composition classroom might be sidestepped, subverted, or—as we might hope—dissolved by liberal values of equal opportunity and fair play, a course integrating the cultural study of gender with rhetoric and composition might be shaped by the following principles.

A PEDAGOGY FOR COMPOSITION AS A CULTURAL PROCESS

Before turning to the specifics of a post-sexist writing course, I want to outline four general principles that might help integrate cultural studies with instruction in composition. Such a course would be dialectical (i.e., politically oppositional), inquiry-driven, cross-disciplinary, and multi-channeled.

The first principle for teaching writing as a cultural practice is that discourse is inherently dialectical and, therefore, political. As V. N. Volosinov put it, "Any real utterance, in one way or another or to one degree or another, makes a statement of agreement with or negation of something" (p. 80). Composing a post-sexist rhetoric begins with the recognition that the sexes are valued differently and that these differences are reproduced, not merely synchronically by language (e.g., the gender specificity in English of singular pronouns) but also by cultural media: verbal discourse, written texts, electronically produced images, and combinations thereof. Media organize the raw data of experience into social and historical narratives about being female or male. These narratives are sexist in that they attribute unequal public capacities and worth to women and men.

There is no way to avoid politics here: to confront social inequities in public discourse for the purpose of redressing them is an overtly political activity. Because most of our students share the dominant patriarchal narratives that underlie gender-biased language, professing a post-sexist rhetoric places the teacher in conflict with his or her students (see Bauer). Engaging students in a rhetorical mode that goes against the cultural grain requires, as Susan Jarratt argues, "overtly confrontational feminist pedagogies as a progressive mode of discourse in the composition classroom" (p. 3). Teaching dialectically, however, does not mean imposing dogma. A political engagement with students is not merely "an extension of the politics of the left," against which Gerald Graff cautions (p. 64). Nevertheless, the pedagogy described here openly confronts not only the existence of social inequity but also a much more volatile issue: how the individual comes to recognize the self in a dominant or subordinate subjectivity.

The second principle for a post-sexist writing course requires that composing grow out of inquiry. In practical terms, this means that research into the cultural intertext must replace "readers." Anthologized readings, no matter how well selected or sophisticated, no longer belong organically to the primary economy of the cultural production. Like a bunch of cut flowers, they have been harvested and consciously arranged for purposes more or less removed from their original rhetorical contexts.

Wherever possible, the pre-texts of student writing should be "primary" sources; research should be as much as possible like fieldwork. Student inquirers should use "secondary" sources, but they must be active construers of knowledge, consciously constructing interpretations to explain the meaning of social life to themselves and others. This focus on composing as an act of interpretation, of making new texts out of the extant cultural pre-text, subverts the traditional research project: writing as the assemblage of cut-and-paste term papers that mimic the dissemination of authorized knowledge in institutional hierarchies. Instead, it gives the students the "textual competence," in Scholes's words (p. 21), the critical and interpretative independence to be active participants in their culture rather than its "insensitive dupes and victims" (xi).

A third principle of composing as a cultural process follows from an inquiry-driven pedagogy: writing and research are cross-disciplinary. Questions of cultural production cut across traditional disciplinary boundaries, but they require answers in the various academic vernaculars of knowledge. In the course of investigating the construction of gender, students borrow as much as possible from the knowledge, nomenclature, and methodologies of the human studies: classifications of social organization, ethnographic methods of observation, functionalist approaches from structural anthropology, mass-communications theory, techniques of film and literary criticism, historiographic conventions of explanation, concepts from religious studies, and much else. In so doing, they learn to respect disciplinary knowledge as tested resources valuable to their own rhetorical ends, rather than as monolithic embodiments of universal truth. Thus, the post-sexist investigation of gender provides a natural interface between the introductory writing course and academic discourses across the curriculum.

The fourth and final principle in taking a cultural approach to the composing process recognizes the centrality of the electronically reproduced image in representational acts. The texts from which students construct their gendered narratives of self are no longer—if they ever were—primarily written. The performance of "pertness" in women or "aggressiveness" in men (the parallel use of which, in their adjectival forms, *Guidelines* proscribes as gender-biased) is a complex social behavior much easier to model pictorially than to describe in words. A post-sexist writing pedagogy borrows from the applied "grammatology" of Gregory Ulmer the notion of "scripting," according to which composition becomes a "multichanneled performance": the image can be translated into written text, while writing can become the "screenplay" for enactment (pp. xii–xiii). The transcription of moving or print images, which for our students are the basic medium of cultural currency, in the same act composes an interpretation and stabilizes the text in letters, facilitating rhetorical analysis. It might be noted as well that studying the imaginary, as always potentially scriptable cultural performances, revives the oratorical and elocutionary dimensions of rhetoric, which are usually absent from contemporary concepts of communication.

SYLLABUS: WRITING, INTERMEDIA, AND INQUIRY

The syllabus that follows was developed for a required, second-semester composition course in which students are expected to learn the techniques of library research, the use of secondary sources, and the conventions of academic discourse. These objectives, I hope to show, are quite compatible with inquiry into the cultural formation of gender, the foundation on which a post-sexist rhetoric must be constructed. The syllabus is divided into four segments: parts I–III require about three weeks each and are devoted to methodology; part IV, consuming the final seven weeks of the semester, applies methods to a major research project.

Part I: The Basics of Academic Inquiry
Assignment 1: Summarizing a Written Source. Read the textbook chapter on summarizing sources. Then, using the on-line catalogue, find an extended definition of "culture" and summarize it.

Assignment 2: Synthesizing Two Sources. Read the chapter on writing a simple synthesis; then find and summarize an extended definition of "gender." Review your definition of "culture" (Assignment 1), looking for similarities that connect the two concepts. Finally, write a synthesis in which you establish the primary relationships between the concepts of culture and gender.

Students work individually on the first two assignments. They familiarize themselves with the library and its various systems of information storage and retrieval, the note-taking process, the determination of what counts as a scholarly source, and the basic interpretive skills of paraphrase and citation necessary to retextualizing written sources. At this stage, they also work on the grammatical, stylistic, and rhetorical refinement of their own writing. In Part II, the focus shifts from individual to collaborative investigation as students work in groups of three or four to develop the critical abilities by which knowledge is constructed socially.

Part II: Dialogue and Knowledge-Making

Assignment 3: Comparison and Critique of Sources. Using individual summaries and syntheses of written sources, each group will construct its own definition of "culture" and "gender." Group definitions will build on—and add to—individual summaries and syntheses, first, by comparing and evaluating and, second, by refining, illustrating, and elaborating them. Group definitions must include a complete annotated bibliography of sources considered by its members.

Assignment 3 is pivotal to the production of a post-sexist rhetoric for two reasons. First, without carefully articulated definitions of culture and gender, students will find it impossible to resist their own ideology. They begin with assumptions about the world and their relation to it that are the common epistemic property of mass youth culture. In Moffatt's words, their "sense of generation"—their situation in society and history—"comes to them through popular music, the movies, TV, and certain mass-market magazines"; and their understanding of culture "only marginally modifies their fundamental individualism" (pp. 32, 151).

In this context, the teacher of cultural studies must struggle constantly and vigilantly to keep one set of signifiers, here "the cultural reproduction of gender," from eliding into the dominant cultural discourse, according to which individuals recognize and voluntarily accept or reject sex roles. To anticipate my conclusion, the dialectical tension between these competing structures of reality is pedagogically healthy: its negotiation demands real intellectual discipline. The give-and-take of conflicting interests out of which the "obvious" takes shape re-creates for both teacher and student the very process by which history has organized our world for us. And this dialectical relationship prevents what critics on the right call political indoctrination—although it does insist that students confront the ideological blind spots of their enculturation, which would not otherwise be visible to them.

A second reason for insisting on the negotiation of precise definitions for the propositional terms driving inquiry (culture and gender) is pedagogical: learning, as Bartholomae and others have insisted, requires learners to "reinvent" the known. Recitation was the formal means by which students reinvented knowledge when knowledge was conceived of as static. In an age of information overload and ethical brownout, we must involve students in helping to determine what should count as knowledge. As Reither and Vipond argue, writing and knowing are "profoundly collaborative processes" (p. 862), and collaborative inquiry is therefore the best approach to giving students the critical distance from which to reconsider the "realities" of the media they consume. In

Assignment3, students appropriate an approach to knowledge by defining the terms of their investigation into gender and media.

Part III: Doing Field Research
   Assignment 4: First, read the assigned chapters [on library reserve] in Michael Arlen's *Sixty Seconds*. Then select a full page ad from a men's or women's magazine—one that suggests a story to you. Finally, write a script for converting your ad's image into a short play, complete with descriptions of setting, props, and characters as well as stage directions and dialogue.

   The basic objective of this assignment is to sensitize students to the fact that images are *re-presentations* of imagination, not windows on reality. The Arlen text, an ethnographic study of the production of AT&T's original "Reach Out and Touch Someone" campaign, provides an inside view of how these representations are constructed. By rematerializing the social production of image/text, the assignment requires students to address what John Trimbur has called "the rhetoric of deproduction," the discursive practices by which, first, propositions are divorced from the objects and artifacts to which they refer and, second, the contingent and culturally mediated nature of this reference is erased. The result is our students' faith in the existence of an objective reality mirrored by an unproblematic, univocal language ("Essayist Literacy," pp. 80–82). The scripting of a text's production helps to reestablish its links to the material conditions of its production. (Arlen makes these links most palpable.)
   In the following assignment, the process is examined from the opposite direction: the class applies the ethnographic technique Clifford Geertz calls "thick description" to the film *Working Girl*. Students formulate a specific question from a list of suggestions focusing attention on the representation of gender in the film (see the appendix). We spend several class periods analyzing the means by which the cinematic narrative works to create an image of man and woman in the world it constructs. Each student contributes evidence gleaned from the focal perspective of the question she or he has selected.
   It should be noted that performing a close reading of a film text is no easier for students than discerning nuances in written texts. Visual details pass unnoticed, and much class time must be invested in close analysis ("thick description") of frozen frames.

Assignment 5: The Narrative as Image. Using evidence from your own "field notes" and those of other class members, explain how Tess's story in *Working Girl* creates an image of what women or men are like.

Part IV of the syllabus, "Representation of Gender in Visual Media," brings together the textual competencies developed in the previous five assignments. Students select a film, television series, or set of print images as the topic of the final research paper. They form research and editing groups based on medium and genre. During the final week of classes, these groups will summarize and synthesize their research for a desktop publication, "Studies in Gender and Media," that I distribute to students at the final exam. The research project is presented in the following terms:

Assignment 6: In examining the construction of gender in the particular visual "text" you have chosen, remember that images—whether still or moving—are *re*-presentations of the physical world (including human sexual differences) and of the society that produces them. The patterns that we see in media are not nature itself but culturally coded interpretations of what nature "is like." The meaning is not already there; it has been put there.

In determining *what* has been put into your text, you will be looking for the answer to the question: Anatomy aside, how are men and women different in the world constructed—"imaged"—by . . . [your text]?

The research paper reporting your investigation of gender and visual media must contain four parts (not necessarily in this order):

1. An extended definition of "gender," drawn from at least two written sources, in which you clearly distinguish it from "sex"
2. A thesis statement clearly articulating the conclusion(s) of your study (for example, "In . . . wo/men are represented as. . . .")
3. A discussion of "representation" in the medium you have chosen, based on a minimum of four sources (two of which must be scholarly), which will support your textual critique and analysis
4. A detailed explication of gender (using "thick description") as represented in your text, carefully deployed in support of your thesis.

TWO WRITERS COMPOSING A POST-SEXIST RHETORIC

Most students first encounter rhetoric as young adults in an introductory composition course. Either explicitly or implicitly they are pointed to a discursive space and taught how to situate themselves in relation to texts, theirs and others, and the field of social reference that texts occupy. The reproduction of orthodox individualism, learned at home, in the schools, and in the media, requires an introductory rhetoric that constructs the writer as an autonomous arbiter of reality, capable of "saying no" to gender-biased language as well as "saying yes" to the conventions of academic discourse. Reigning expressivist and cognitivist rhetorics teach students to construct just such a relationship between self and "audience."

A post-sexist rhetoric, by contrast, insists that both writer and audience share a cultural subjectivity that has effectively "naturalized" gender. Because of these blind spots (which might as well be called ideological), the focus of inquiry must shift from the world, where women and men are the way they really are, to the media, which re-create the naturalness of the way things really are. I want to discuss briefly the inquiry into representation of gender conducted by two students who worked through the syllabus described above.

Terri's research paper, "Sex-Role Stereotyping in Children's Cartoons," examined the construction of gender in children's television programming. After defining "gender" and discussing its relationship to cultural media, Terri reviewed the scholarly literature, choosing Richard Levinson's 1976 content analysis of Saturday morning cartoons as the point of departure. She then presented her own research, the "fieldwork" she had done in the "Saturday morning ghetto" (as Levinson phrased it) of children's cartoons.

On two consecutive Saturdays, Terri taped episodes of programs including "Josie and the Pussycats," "Scooby Do," and "The Flintstones Comedy Hour." She then transcripted the representations of males and females in her pictorial texts, focusing in particular on "changes [since Levinson's study, 1976] in the ways that television cartoons portrayed female characters." At first, she hypothesized that the cartoons would reflect the progress toward equality that she believed had taken place in the last fifteen years. "What I found was that women were given more freedom to do things, other than be maids and housewives, than they had in the 1970s, but their relationship to the male characters was still the same." In one episode of "Josie," for example, Valerie (the program's only black) "engineered the major rescue by programming a robot to become an ally against the villain." Valerie piloted the group's spaceship, but she was the only female character observed at the controls of a vehicle: "females rarely drive any vehicle when males are available."

The most common relationships between boys and girls in the cartoons Terri studied were romantic: "Not much has changed since Olive Oyl." Polly, of "Sweet Polly Purebread," fell into the clutches of a villain and required rescuing by the hero, as did Melody in "Josie." When not in need of rescue, the girls in the cartoons often plotted to "catch" or "trap" boys. Terri described three instances that occurred during the two-hour observation. Other major preoccupations of females included "nagging, complaining, wanting things, or in the case of Alexandra [on "Josie"] just talking until someone put a bag over her head." In her conclusion, Terri wrote: "The sex roles in the cartoon programs continue to emphasize tradition and sexism. Young people are not likely to gain any insight into the new roles and perceptions that many women have of themselves or want for their daughters today."

In "The Quiet Inner Strength of Women: *The African Queen*," Shawn examined John Huston's classic film as a representation of the "common belief that women have the inner strength and endurance to hold men, families, and societies together . . . in such a way that the male is never made to feel inferior or put down by this strength of a woman." The Hepburn character, Rose Sayer, is "the perfect role model for women to act as men's social crutch." Shawn analyzes in detail the mediary role Rose plays, first between her unctuous missionary brother and the two-fisted, hard-drinking Charlie Allnut (Humphrey Bogart) and, for most of the film, between Charlie and the vicissitudes of their journey downriver.

Shawn's reading focuses on the position of the protagonists in relation to each other and to other characters. She diagrams a number of pivotal scenes in addition to transcribing the dialogue, voices, expressions, and gestures. In one scene, for example, Rose hits on the idea of making torpedoes to blow up the German boat *Louisa*:

The camera stays on Charlie as he laughs and tells her that she is being ridiculous. But then she becomes excited and begins to move forward and gesture with her hands. She wrinkles her forehead in a puzzled way and asks him questions about how to make torpedoes which he knows the answers to. Once he is convinced by her that the idea will work, she then becomes stern and ladylike again. Her face relaxes and she moves to the background again.

In sequences like this, Shawn locates the representation of woman as "social crutch," as she calls it: "Rose exudes strength and courage that she cleverly gives to Charlie . . . by optimism, small compliments and feminine gestures of helplessness. This is shown most clearly in her movements forward and back in the scene."

RESOLVING THE CONFLICT IN GENDERED REPRESENTATION

Terri and Shawn both put their fingers on the representational pulse of gender-biased stereotypes proscribed by their university's official policy against patronizing and stereotypical references to women. *Guidelines* admonishes: "Avoid the stereotypes of the logical, objective male and the emotional, subjective female. Women should not be portrayed as helpless nor be made the figures of fun or objects of scorn." The female figure in the childrens's cartoons Terri studied is "the little woman," and Shawn's Rose Sayer character is certainly "the better half," both expressions labeled "biased terms" by the *Guidelines*.

Cultural studies, nevertheless, do not produce epiphanies. The post-sexist pedagogy described here offers students an alternative means of constructing experience of gender, an opportunity to rethink in a disciplined way their relationship to the world, reimagining experience as subject to history and culture rather than as a series of objective choices made by autonomous individuals. The writing instructor can show students how to resist dominant cultural formations like gender; but he or she cannot overcome students' inherent acquiescence in them. The instructor can open up the discursive space—a post-sexist rhetoric—for a critique of dominant narratives of gender; but students can be counted on to resist significant revisions of their own personal stories.

I have advanced the claim that the pedagogical attempt to compose a post-sexist rhetoric is inherently dialectical because it assigns students to resist their own cultural subjectivity. The other pole of the dialectic is the students' resistance to this assignment. Dale Bauer has pointed to the "critical tension" that the politically committed feminist teacher inevitably faces in the classroom. In their inquiry into the representation of gender, my students felt compelled to resolve the tension between their ideology of equal opportunity and the asymmetries of power and worth they discovered and documented in their research.

Students' resistance to the subjectivity of gender—their determination to resolve the conflict between the egalitarian discourse of American individualism and the pervasive evidence of inequities—employs a number of recurring and interrelated rhetorical strategies. These strategies, doubtless familiar to regular readers of student writing, include the doctrines of *separate* (but equal) *spheres*, the public sphere for men, the private one for women; of *social meliorism*, according to which things were bad in the past but are getting better; and of *demonology*, the belief that social inequities are the result of a few bad people or institutions that can be distinguished from "society." (These rhetorical moves will be discussed in a little more detail in a later chapter.)

Terri's study of children's television programs resolves the conflict between her ideology and her evidence in much the same way: her own text constructs a world fully formed and independent of its linguistic representation. We can glimpse this strategy in her judgment about the cartoons' not offering children "any *insight* into the new roles and perceptions that women have of themselves or want for their daughters today" (emphasis added). Terri creates a world for the new roles and perceptions, accessible by *insight*, thereby circumventing the biased, stereotypical representations of sex in the "old" world of children's television.

In the concluding sentence of her research paper, Terri claims that her study has "raised serious questions about television's *accuracy* of sex role representations" (emphasis added). She has finally shifted the problem from the inertia of cultural reproduction—which she herself identifies in the stereotypical representations of the cartoons—to a simpler reality that television programming ought to reflect more *accurately*. Terri has thereby harmonized the dissonance between her evidence of inequality and her faith in the "reality" of social equality.

The strategy of *naturalization*, the collapse of distinctions between culture and nature, takes *vulgar realism* one step farther. Anything that goes on in the world that students refer to as reality is *natural*. As a result, they have a hard time distinguishing between sex, patently an objective characteristic existing in the "real world," and gender, a cultural formation that ascribes meaning to biological identity but is a quality of subjective experience. Without a clear concept of cultural subjectivity, students often represent gender as a behavior "learned," by observation and mimesis, from "society." Gender is thereby reduced to a set of objective characteristics that the subject must consciously learn to match with her or his physiology. And if gender is learned, it can also be mislearned. In the course of defining gender, a number of students speculated that homosexual identity was a willful, voluntary decision to learn the wrong, the *unnatural*, gender role.

This ideological impetus to naturalize and to intentionalize gender pervades Shawn's paper; it is always ready to help her subvert her attempt to understand the film as a cultural production. There is a constant tension between her sense that she is watching the subtle replication of androcentrism (woman as "social crutch") and her representation of Rose's "quiet inner strength" as a reflection of woman's *natural* responsibility for social cohesion. At one point, she observes that the "classic" status of the film tells us something about what Americans "really believe about relationships." Elsewhere, she wonders if she isn't "reading too much into" what "could just be a story about two people." Her paper is marked by numerous signs of the epistemic struggle between two modes of explaining sexual identity: the autonomous and the cultural.

In her conclusion, Shawn finally resolves this dialectical tension. *The African Queen* becomes "a remake of what we all know as the real world." The discursive space, opened up by the assignment, is closed again, laying to rest the problem of social inequity by *naturalizing* the woman's performance as "social crutch" and as mirror of male egoism.

The pedagogy outlined here introduces students to the conventions of academic research and writing; it also introduces them to the study of culture. Our students, like most Americans, lack a theory of subject formation. They explain their experiences to themselves in terms of autonomous individuals freely choosing their identities as they would fashion themselves from the copious outlet malls of consumer capitalism. The work on composing a post-sexist rhetoric is a first step in overcoming this deeply ingrained cultural narrative of autonomy and autogenesis. And it is the first step as well to eliminating gender bias from university discourses.

APPENDIX

Suggested questions to guide research into the representation of gender and media:

Who looks at whom, and how? What does the camera's position—our eye— focus attention on? What is left at the margins or not pictured at all (and why not)?

What contacts—eye or touch—are made? By whom? Under what circumstances? With what response?

Who speaks, to whom, in what tone? Who curses, cries, screams, laughs, etc.?

How are people physically positioned in relation to each other and to objects? What gestures, "body language," are displayed?

Who smiles, glowers, etc.? Are these expressions coded as "natural" or manipulative?

Who refers to the body, whose body, and how? Who grooms, under what circumstances, and how?

What's the costume: dress, ornament, jewelry? What physical objects (or props) are characters associated with?

Who takes their clothes off, and under what conditions? How do clothes enable or restrict action?

What activities do the characters engage in or avoid? What are their goals? And how do they try to accomplish them?

Who's good at what task? Who's incompetent, bumbling?

What work do the characters do? How do they get things? What is their (apparent) relationship to the world outside the camera's eye?

What do the characters desire? Fear? Value?

What's funny, to whom, and why?

Chapter 4

Radical Pedagogy and Student Resistance: Can We Fight the Power?

CO-AUTHORED WITH KAREN FITTS

These are trying times for those attempting to teach writing as a critical, rhetorically sophisticated engagement with questions of language and power. In the first place, many in the academy continue to believe, honestly or strategically, that teaching writing can and ought to be a politically neutral process. And recently, conflicts over the pathology and prognosis of institutionalized social inequities (particularly those of race and gender) have been portrayed by conservatives—and those in the press who understand that anti-intellectualism is good copy in America—as evidence of a radical academic fifth column. This new Red Scare of "political correctness" has frightened even that stalwart of rhetoric and composition studies Maxine Hairston, who has condemned "turning . . . [the] composition course into a forum for debate on social issues" ("Required Writing," p. 1). Teachers of rhetoric and writing should avoid political controversies, Hairston argues, because students are not interested in them and instructors lack "expertise" in "complex psychological and social problems" like racism and sexism. She believes that grade-conscious students will simply "parrot" their instructors' opinions on controversial issues (p. 1).

To be clear from the outset, we write in this essay from a "politically correct" standpoint in the sense that that term is understood on the right and in the popular press. Our politics are materialist-feminist, and they are central to our pedagogical and professional ethos. It is important to us, for example, that our teaching practices actively challenge the white, middle-class consensus that Americans can afford to ignore the poverty strangling inner-city social life, the general erosion of women's reproductive rights, and the growing ecological threat of Western technologies. We share with other "politically correct" academics the concern that democratic and liberatory ideals of a university education are increasingly reduced to "disciplines" that will make Americans more productive in the workplace.

Nevertheless, as professors of rhetoric, we are also committed to open democratic forums, free expression of conflicting arguments, and an empathic classroom environment for our students' apprenticeship in the public discourse of self-governance. We are, in short, as opposed to the institution of "thought police" as any conservative critic of "political correctness." But unlike those on the right, we do not believe that writing can be separated from politics, that there are ideologically neutral topics that students can write about. Hairston's insistence that students write about "their own ideas" merely confirms the ideology of privatization that shepherds students away from questions of social equity unpalatable to beneficiaries of the status quo.

The issue, simply put, is this: Can the writing instructor, inevitably committed to some ideological position or another, cultivate an open and honest dialogue about public events? Or, in other words, does fairness require limiting the topoi of composition classes to the supposedly personal or objective so that students are not forced to bend the knee to their teachers' political agendas?

In order to be ethical, instructors should articulate their political commitments; furthermore, when governed by sound pedagogical practice, this approach is a great advantage to students of rhetoric and writing. In the first place, teaching rhetoric requires "modeling" political advocacy. And advocacy itself is necessary to any dialogue—to any authentic, and therefore rhetorical, exchange. In fact, we will argue that the dialectical exchange anticipated by a "forensic" (Sloane) or "sophistic" (Jarratt) pedagogy actually precludes the one-sided imposition of "truth" or "political correctness" that critics on the right fear.

There are two basic reasons why political advocacy should be considered an appropriate rhetorical stance for teaching rhetoric in introductory writing courses. The first has to do with the rhetorical nature of truth claims. As Thomas Sloane maintains, all discourse is one or another kind of argument, and the forensic approach to establishing truth is "paradigmatic of rhetorical thinking itself" (468). It aims at discovering stasis: the point at issue, "the precise point on which the dispute seems to turn" (466). The discovery of stasis, as Richard Fulkerson suggests, proceeds by interrogating a claim as if it were a prima facie case presented at law: "the case (extended argument) made for a claim is structurally and substantively complete so that if no counter-case were presented then the claim would stand" (448).

Approaching an argument's point of stasis means exhausting, as nearly as possible, all the perspectives—not just binary, pro-and-con "sides"— into which arguments have been conventionally sedimented. In this sense, stasis is a critical method appropriate to rhetorical invention and analysis in much the same way poststructural literary theory is suited to "discovering" or inventing critical readings of literary texts. It isolates or "freezes" the topos, allowing the writer to observe minutely the social, cultural, and psychological implications of its claim to veracity. This technique encourages students to step back and walk around a proposition, examining its construction and looking, in particular, for the gaps and fissures, the telltale signs of covert interests, dogmas, and desires. The instructor's job is to keep the complex process bubbling, and for this reason political advocacy is a valuable catalyst. Avoiding political issues as Hairston counsels, even if possible, would fail to engage students in those very rhetorical practices that articulate and validate knowledge.

The second reason why "political correctness" in the writing classroom poses no threat to academic freedom is the inexorable and protean operation of culture, which we refer to loosely as ideology. Our own experience indicates that Hairston's fears—that students will merely learn to "parrot" the political rectitude of their writing teachers—are largely without basis, if for no other reason than that students find ways (invent rhetorical strategies, as we will call it) to subvert or resist oppositional pedagogies. We would first like to explore the operation of ideological resistance in our own writing classes, returning at the end of this chapter to a brief discussion of stasis-seeking pedagogy at work as classroom praxis.

Over the last several semesters, we have attempted to make our classrooms the scene for confronting cultural practices that replicate social inequities. Our objective, therefore, has been to awaken students to the role of culture in giving meaning to—or overlaying with significance— female or male physiology, to use a prominent example. In short, we consider our role to be that of *teaching resistance* to cultural definitions of biological sex by provoking dissonance between egalitarian expectations, on the one hand, and social and cultural asymmetries of power and worth, on the other. We have developed a number of assignments to accomplish this project.

In one assignment we have used, small groups of students research gender in non-Western societies, reporting to the class on the cultural differences they detect. The aim here is to denaturalize and relativize students' own understanding of sexual difference. A second assignment asks students to investigate the ways in which gender restricts or expands people's lives. Our hope is that as they inquire into "real world" social practices—athletics, police work, the arts, domestic arrangements, and domestic violence—they will discover that inequities exist and that they may well be rooted in gender.

Another assignment that we have found most provocative of the "critical tension" Dale Bauer recommends to feminist teachers (391) asks students to examine the *visual* representation of gender in a specific cultural text of their own selection—film, print advertising, record album art, and the like. In class, we practice the use of "thick description" and script narratives of textual diegesis. Student research often draws on the growing body of work in film criticism and the rhetoric of advertising, which are most often informed by feminist theory. Inquiry like this, we have come to believe, problematizes these visual representations, helping students to distinguish nature (sex) from culture (gender). The object of their research and criticism is for the students to answer this question: "Anatomy aside, how are men and women different in the world constructed—or imaged—by your text?"

The purpose of these pedagogical practices is to give students the critical ability to recognize and to resist the flood of visual media in which we are all immersed and that to a significant degree determine our identities. Electronic media place an entire ideological apparatus, including the control of visual representations of gender, in the hands of the entertainment and advertising industries. Under this regime, to quote Annette Kuhn, "subjectivity is always gendered and every human being is, and remains, either male or female. . . . Moreover, in ideology gender identity is not merely absolute: it also lies at the very heart of human subjectivity" (52). This is an enormous institutional power over our students, and because it is used to reproduce sexual inequality and stereotypes, we believe that literacy must include a critical awareness of how subjects become gendered in an age of electronic images.

As we began to analyze student responses to our assignments, we noticed that they often invented ways (some rather subtle) to resist the conclusions of their own inquiries. That is, they invented rhetorical strategies to reconcile their findings to the ideology of sexual difference that the assignments were calculated to problematize. An awareness of these strategies, or of the directions that students' contentions are liable to take, assisted our goal of calling up an alternative worldview. In any case, however, it became increasingly clear that our pedagogy—conceived of as oppositional—had indeed become a dialectical process. We had set out to teach students a construction of reality that *we* find just and compelling; but the students, for the most part, clung to the essentialist realities authorized by the dominant culture.

Before we explore the basis of this *aporia*, a statement of pedagogical credo seems in order. We believe that our students, like most Americans lacking a theory of subject formation, cannot adequately account for the influence of culture on the individual. And to paper over this theoretical absence, they must posit the existence of an autonomous self. Since we will be critiquing this vitalist rhetoric with citations from student texts, we risk presenting ourselves as privileged subjects, somehow standing outside culture. How did our understanding of sexual difference escape the dominant culture that we oppose? The short answer is—we suppose—that our own subjectivity results from the accidental confluence of social forces on our lives, which subverted to some degree the dominant gender patterns and demanded some egalitarian ones. Thus, the internal contradictions of our personal histories have situated us at the critical margin. And it is from this critical margin that we engage our students.

As suggested above, we have discovered that students deploy a number of recurring and interrelated rhetorical strategies to avoid confronting the subjectivity of gender, as opposed to the objective nature of biological sex. We will list these strategies briefly and then illustrate them with specific applications in student texts.

1. Objectification: There exist in nature various objective categories like separate spheres (the public realm for men, the private realm for women).
2. Social meliorism: In the past, things were bad, but they are getting better.
3. Pragmatism: Solving specific problems—like ending discrimination in the workplace—will lead to sexual equality.
4. Demonology: Oppression and exploitation of women are the result of a few bad people or institutions that can be distinguished from "society."
5. Individual autonomy ("freedom of choice"): We can "just say no" to stereotypes and inequities.

It should be pointed out that the student papers we will be quoting from are not the failures, the inferior work of poorer students that is easy to cite invidiously, but the efforts of "strong" writers who understand what is at stake and who are insisting on their own construction of the world—the dominant one that we are opposing.

We will begin with objectification. Our students still inhabit a world of Cartesian dualism. The result is that they have a hard time distinguishing between sex, patently an objective characteristic existing in the "real world," and gender, a cultural formation that ascribes meaning to biological identity but is a quality of subjective experience. Without a clear concept of cultural subjectivity, our students often rendered sex and gender as distinct but complementary qualities, the former ascribed by birth, the latter "learned," most often by observation and mimesis, from "society." The continual blurring of biology and culture reduces gender to a set of objective characteristics that the subject must consciously learn to match with her or his physiology. Gender itself thus becomes an objective category. And this, as we hope to show, opens up the space for the privileged subject of experience—the self.

This "naturalization" of gender caused one student, in an essay examining homophobia, to speculate in these words:

Some individuals are born with a gender problem. They are brought up . . . in a way that goes against proper gender traits, *sexually* a male or female but gender-wise the opposite. Our society still believes that a man should be a man and a woman should be a woman. If the sex of a person conflicts with the gender of that person, operations can be done to alter the problem.

In this case, clarification of the blurred categories seems to require surgery. More commonly, it entails the recognition of separate, and unequal, spheres for men and women. The underlying conviction repeatedly surfaced that men's physical strength determined their dominance in public life and as providers, while women's "weakness" and their physiological role in procreation determined their subordination to the domestic sphere. In a paper on gender roles in a native Alaskan society, for example, a student writes that "the men work" (they go on hunting expeditions lasting up to six months) while "the women stay at home with the children." Staying at home turns out to include all kinds of work essential to the group's survival: fishing, making and repairing tools, and trapping and butchering seals. However, the student imposes her own culturally determined understanding of the natural order—including the denigration of women's work—on the cultural arrangements she was investigating, *even though*, by the student's own evidence, that work was highly valued by the group under consideration.

In terms of students' interpretive strategies, the objectification of cultural productions makes for a more or less simplistic realism. Because objects exist "out there" in nature, students have difficulty distinguishing between "representation" (which is constructed) and "reflection" (which implies a direct access to nature). They often use the words interchangeably. In a study of how representation of women on television programs "reinforce[s] our definition of gender," a student concludes:

Because television needs to be realistic, sometimes it goes too far and isn't representative of our society. On TV, women that have important executive jobs can stay late at work and don't worry about a family when, realistically, most women do have to come home to a family.

Here, even though the student announces the influence of the media in reinforcing gender, as she puts it, she still holds on to a naive realism according to which television must reflect or "keep up" with objective social changes (from "The Donna Reed Show" to "Growing Pains") but not get too far ahead and thereby "misrepresent" the reality of women's changing roles.

This text provides a bridge to the second rhetorical strategy our students use to bring their knowledge into line with their ideology: social meliorism. No matter how bad the world revealed to them by research, students are ready to find that it is getting better. The idea of progress is a venerable and distinctly American response to social problems, and we find that students use it consistently. Most papers, no matter how critical of the status quo, conclude on an upbeat note. A young woman writing on what she calls "the good old boys' club" of television newscasting, concludes with these words:

If the television news industry starts now, perhaps it can catch up with all the other professions and realize that women can be just as serious, capable, and intelligent as men. Maybe even more so.

Another student, examining the coverage of the 1988 Winter Olympics, "found plenty of babble on women's appearance, their unhappy personal lives, their vulnerabilities and jealousies." Nevertheless, she concludes that "Attitudes towards women's involvement in sports is becoming more positive, [and] the perception of women athletes is also improving." When students take such a stance, their commitment to social activism or to the individual's responsibility for political action is significantly eroded because they feel that time itself will somehow improve conditions.

The discovery of progress in the flow of events is closely related to a third tactic students use to harmonize the dissonance between what they find and what they believe: pragmatism. The most deeply embedded cultural inequities are cast as "problems" to be solved. This technique appears most commonly in student investigations of the "second-shift" conflicts faced by working women. One student sees the solution as teaching "husbands to get involved with the kids and housework," which can be done by "encouraging the children of the present time that they can play with anything they want to, such as dolls or pretend kitchens." Although this strategy is certainly laudable, we would argue that what children want to play with is determined by complex social forces unresponsive to pragmatic intervention. A male child, for instance, experiencing the profound force the media can bring to bear, is not likely to abandon "male" identity (packaged in the form of G.I. Joe, etc.) at the urging of his mother, a devalued agent in contemporary culture.

Students often contend that inequities, discrimination, and harassment in the workplace can be overcome by winning the respect of colleagues or demonstrating competence to the public. After noting the set arrangement and gestures that subordinate "Today Show"'s Deborah Norville to her male colleagues and her assignment to "softer" stories like premature babies and National Secretaries Day, a student concludes:

Due to our culture, women are perceived as being weaker and more emotional than men. . . . Until [they] are able to convince the public that they are capable of reporting "hard" news stories, they will be limited in their advancement to the top positions on the television news.

Once the problem of public perception is solved, the student implies, women will be treated equitably. This is probably true, of course, but it fails to consider the monumental cultural transformation involved in changing public perception.

If things are getting better, either because of a natural law of progress or because of the solution of specific problems, students must still account for much that is wrong in the present. The most common rhetorical strategy for this ideological theodicy is demonology. This move is most often associated with student analyses of advertising or the rock music industry. In a study of jeans advertisements, for example, a student finds that the exploitation of women in Calvin Klein, Jordache, and Guess ads "has a negative influence on our culture." Advertisers' exploitation of women in these ads as "seductresses and sexual playthings . . . makes women appear cheap and easy, [and] humiliates them in society." The student conceives of the ads as moral corrosives attacking—"fraudulently," as the student puts it—the society to which they pander. The notion that that society itself produces as well as consumes the ads is missing entirely from the otherwise incisive analysis. The student conjures up a vision of middle America as basically pristine; in other words, Mom and Dad and the folks back on

Poplar Street are not implicated. Sexism can be safely ignored as the product of a few reprehensible sociopaths.

Another student follows the same logic in her genuinely disturbing inquiry into violence and sadism in rock lyrics like those of 2Live Crew. The author laments the passing of clean-cut "teenie bopper groups" and the rise of music "that contains very corrupting messages. Satanism, sex, rape, drug and alcohol abuse, and suicide are just a few of the [messages] that are being sent to innocent and impressionable kids by heavy metal and other groups." Again, the larger social context that governs the production as well as the reception of these messages is not considered.

Finally, we want to consider the most ubiquitous—and the most obvious—rhetorical strategy that students use to contain the political implications of their findings: the positing of an autonomous self capable of being insulated from the corruptions of social life. The ideology of individualism, like the subject-object split that is its philosophical basis, has already been implicit in our categories of social meliorism, pragmatism, and demonology. We will conclude, therefore, with a few examples of the form it has taken in our students' work.

Cultural formation—especially gender—is commonly represented in student discourse not as a set of axes intersecting at the point of the individual subject but as "learned gender roles." This formulation is common in the sources our students use in their papers, and it is not surprising, therefore, that they frequently separate the "actor" from the role he or she learns. As a result, student texts reconstruct for themselves an inner and autonomous self as the player who can choose whether to play assigned cultural roles. Thus, a student writes: "Gender refers to the psychological, social, and cultural components of a person's upbringing *and* how that person identifies himself [*sic*] as a male or female."

Another student writes that "a child is taught to think, feel, and act in ways considered natural, morally appropriate, and desirable for a person of that sex. [With these] lessons we learn to achieve a given gender." Notice that the movement from the cultural subject ("a child") to the self within is marked by the movement from third to first person ("we"). For the student, the shift in person might well represent the desired distancing of the self—the defense of his autonomy—from the necessity of cultural subjectivity.

In terms of the politics of gender, the pervasiveness of individualism is decidedly conservative because it obviates the need for social change. As one student put it with uncharacteristic bluntness: "We all agree change is necessary, but . . . we can begin to change society's attitudes only by changing our own personal attitudes [first]." Another writes somewhat despairingly, in concluding an inquiry into the social significance of blondness, "Women have always been objects or showpieces simply to be looked at. We cannot deny the fact that we have no one to blame for these stereotypes except for ourselves. We created them, and now we will have to destroy them."

From our politically interested perspective, therefore, the efforts to get students thinking in terms of cultural subjectivity instead of individual autonomy were apparently in vain. The "critical tension"—the oppressive identity that Jennifer, the student quoted immediately above, blames on herself—has been relieved or recuperated by the culturally predominant rhetoric of individualism. But from Jennifer's perspective the assignment is a success. In the course of constructing her argument (of achieving stasis), she had been compelled repeatedly to reconfigure her experience in terms of opposing (i.e., feminist) interlocutors, her instructor, and several class members. She finally came to rest at a point, a "structurally and substantively complete" claim, that represents her own prima facie case for individual autonomy. Jennifer has, to warp the legal metaphor, returned the ball to our court. To continue the dialogue, her instructor would have to make a case against the individual's ability to "destroy" stereotypes.

In our classes, we strive to create environments in which the negotiation of truth claims provides a continual source of critical tension. Our pedagogy is inquiry-driven; we avoid providing the authority for arguments. The instructor's role is stubbornly sophistic; we remain sideline coaches, joining in only to stir up contention when students begin to fall over themselves in agreeing with each other. Students, individually and in research groups of three or four, present their claims with supporting evidence to the class. Participation in this public forum often brings changes in both speakers and audience. The speakers begin to anticipate their classmates' counterarguments and to recognize them as significant to their purpose. The audience gains an understanding of its role in pressing "experts," or knowledgeable authorities, for the evidence on which their claims rest. As a result, the major research projects, in final form, generally reflect more careful analysis and authorial responsibility than might otherwise have been the case.

Typical of this process is a student's investigation of "welfare abuse." In her first presentation to the class, the student argued that public assistance programs often support people who are too lazy to work and who want a cushy lifestyle. Some of her classmates, who had first- or secondhand knowledge of cash assistance, medical assistance, food stamps, or job training, countered her claim that "anyone can get a job who is willing to work" and challenged her to examine the economic conditions made possible by welfare. As a result of this response to her first presentation, she visited the public assistance offices in downtown Philadelphia, acquired pamphlets on types of aid available, and interviewed staff workers. She constructed a budget for a family consisting of an unmarried woman with two school-age children and attempted to make the assistance meet the family's most basic needs. By semester's end, she wrote the following:

A stereotypical folklore story often cites the example of the welfare mother driving up to the district office in her Mercedes Benz to pick up welfare checks. This has caused the general public to condemn people on welfare as lazy, unmotivated, and system cheaters. The truth is, though, that public assistance programs provide only the minimum survival level for individuals in need.

Student-led argument necessitated by forensic pedagogy impelled this student to modify her claims significantly. Her project clarified for her, as well as for the students who contested her claims, not only the issue of "welfare abuse" but also the larger interactive, or dialogic, process of asserting claims to knowledge.

Lest it appear that we see students change each time in the direction of "political correctness," we should mention the student who determined, following his semester-long research, that a "man's movement" is needed. We are comfortable with the fact, in spite of the instructor's opposing arguments, the student was able to build a consensus among his classmates for his prima facie case.

Far from stifling the free exchange of ideas, therefore, political advocacy—in the context of a forensic or stasis-seeking pedagogy—facilitates and enriches the dialogue of writing classes. We would agree with Thomas Sloane that advocacy and resistance are the very nature of rhetorical practice. In the struggle to advance our own political agenda against our students' resistance, we have found a way to create a space, an occasion, and a method for cultivating public discourse.

Chapter 5

Teaching the Dialectics of "Objective" Discourse: A Progressive Approach to Business and Professional Writing

With the proliferation of upper-level preprofessional composition courses and writing-across-the-curriculum programs, most writing instructors are likely to be asked to teach technical or business writing in some form or other. Because of widespread notions that these courses should amount to formal training in the pragmatics of institutional information processing, writing instructors committed to fundamental social change may feel serious ethical qualms about teaching these so-called practical courses in business, technical, and professional writing. This was my own concern several years ago when I was first assigned to teach a business writing course: to teach writing without its political context seemed not only dull but dishonest.

There are, of course, obvious theoretical factors militating against "politicizing" supposedly objective writing courses. The orthodox theory of communication insists that discourse is a set of conventions and that learning to write means learning to conform. Some "epistemic" theorists even take the position that knowledge itself is a familiarity not merely with a disciplinary paradigm but also with an institutional dialect or vernacular. Knowledge, then, in Kenneth Bruffee's words, "is identical with the symbol system (i.e., language) in which it is formulated," and each "community of knowledgeable peers . . . constructs knowledge by justifying it socially, that is by arriving at a sort of consensus" ("Social Construction," 779). Freed and Broadhead have illustrated how this process of conformity to conventional discourse works in the actual practice of two international corporations. Written or unwritten "sacred texts" govern the bid proposal process at both Alpha and Omega, the pseudonyms used for an accounting and a management consulting firm. "However unseen they may be," Freed and Broadhead conclude, "the norms define the writer's discourse community, a context that conditions, governs, and constrains, not just the message, but the writer producing it" (162).

In theory, writing that emphasizes convention and conformity seems ideally suited to indoctrinating our writing students in—at best—a kind of active obedience to the demands of corporate bureaucracies. The practice this theory implies requires us to train our students to meet the information-processing needs of employers, at the same time silencing or at least ignoring any criticism of the status quo.

To make matters worse (from the dissident standpoint), students are increasingly encouraged to take technical and preprofessional writing courses in place of traditional liberal arts electives, which at least suggest a critical distance from the ideology of corporate capitalism. Writing courses that college catalogs like to describe as "practical" too often emphasize "forms and techniques" of documents rather than the rhetorical analysis and critical evaluation of "real-world" discursive practices, which always incorporate material conflicts and their ideological, "interested" vindication.

The demand for career-oriented writing skills courses is no doubt the academic backwash of the rising conservative tide in American politics. It seems related as well to the persistence of positivism: the whole idea of "practical" implies the existence of a real object-world, where forms and techniques are efficacious but mere theory and politics are not, as the pragmatic philosopher Richard Rorty likes to say, "profitable topics" ("Pragmatism," 61). The ideal of objectivity in discourse presupposes a domain of experience that is suprapolitical, value-free, and directly accessible through representational signification. This circling of the wagons around the pragmatic "objectivity" of corporate capitalism tends to divide our profession into "settlers and Indians." I cannot in good conscience divide teaching into technique and ethical commitment to socioeconomic equality.

Fortunately, recent work in rhetoric has begun to undermine the widespread theoretical support for teaching conservative ideology as the necessary pedagogy of business and technical writing courses. Greg Myers, for example, has pointed out the common ideology of the two kinds of rhetorical appeals, the "appeal to the authority of consensus" and the "appeal to the authority of reality," which at first glance seem to be contradictory: those who argue that reality is a social construction offer us no way "to criticize this construct. Having discovered the role of consensus

Dialectics of "Objective" Discourse   65

in the production of knowledge, [they take] this consensus as something that just is," instead of recognizing the role of social and economic factors in the construction of so-called realities ("Reality," 166–67).

More recently, the belief that learning—the appropriation of knowledge—is identical with conforming to the conventions of an authoritative discourse has been disputed by Thomas O. Sloane from the epistemological perspective of classical (Ciceronian) forensic *inventio*. Far from being the result of consensus, Sloane argues, knowledge is hammered out through disputation by the discovery—or better, the uncovering—of stasis, "the precise point on which the dispute seems to turn" (466). And Thomas Kent has argued that language is not inherently conventional, that it "does not represent a superstructure built on convention; [instead] language provides the base on which a superstructure of conventions resides" (505). Good rhetoricians must eternally remind us that only language (as cultural medium) creates the reality of the objective world.

A theoretical rationale exists, therefore, for a critical approach to teaching technical and institutional writing. According to this argument, processing and analyzing discourse are better conceived as active resistance to, rather than passive acquisition of, the authority of conventions. Institutional discourse—the employee training manual as well as the bid proposal—becomes a move in the struggle to preserve wealth, power, and the political system that has apportioned them in favor of the institution's hierarchy in the first place.

In the remainder of this chapter, I would like to describe a pedagogical strategy that accomplishes the practical aims of courses variously labeled as technical, business, and professional writing, and at the same time offers students the opportunity to recognize and critique the ideology of institutional discourses.

TEACHING PREPROFESSIONAL WRITING DIALECTICALLY

Since upper-level writing courses at most colleges and universities increasingly emphasize conformity to the conventions of institutional discourse, business or technical writing assignments tend to be formulaic, hypothetical "problem-solving" exercises calling on students to assume the subordinate roles they will fill as employees. A dialectical pedagogy rejects casting students in these roles by requiring them to undertake ethnographic research into the actual use of writing in a technical or organizational application. Praxis is, after all, a far more "practical" approach to writing instruction than learning to imitate hypostatized forms of reports, proposals, and memoranda. And the use of textbook material—even as rhetorical models—perpetuates and legitimizes authoritarian attitudes toward writing as labor.

The notion that there is some Platonic ideal for a "good" memo (or anything else) dies slowly, but it can in fact be dispatched. The best way to get rid of it is to require students to investigate, analyze, and critique the function of writing in the real-world context of work. To be really practical, therefore, we need to require our students to confront the actual texts of institutional practice.

At the beginning of the semester, I ask students to form small (three to five members) interest groups and to formulate a topic and conduct research for a collaborative project. The groups are to complete two major investigative projects during the term, each culminating in an individual written case study and a group oral presentation to the rest of the class. In the course of their research, students focus increasingly on a specific written interchange in the particular part of the power/knowledge network they have chosen to study. They write formal proposals for their individual case studies, collect illustrative documents and present them to the rest of the class, interview those who actually compose institutional discourse, write periodic progress reports, and record all of their work in a research log.

In order to assure a genuinely dialectical approach to the writing process, however, I further instruct students to choose topics with a clear potential for conflict. The syllabus for my business writing course puts it this way:

In a complex, interdependent society like ours, business writing, like any purposeful activity, is undertaken to advance someone's interests, often at the expense of someone else's. In choosing your research project, be on the lookout for conflicting interests. If you study the process by which a company disposes of solid wastes, for example, look at the process from the perspective of those whose interests are directly and indirectly in conflict with the company's: dump site neighbors, the local municipality, state or federal "watchdog" agencies, and environmentalist groups. Remember, for every dump*er* there is a dump*ee*.

An assignment like this is intended to emphasize the centrality of conflict to the business world and the consequent necessity for understanding rhetorical principles and their application to business writing. Once students understand how conflict underpins the writing process of business discourse, they can begin to understand that knowledge is never merely "reflected" or presented objectively in business documents. Instead, such documents materialize the social conflict inherent in a system of commodity production that maximizes the extraction of surplus value from its environment, natural and human.

WINCHESTER: A CASE STUDY IN THE RHETORIC OF REAL ESTATE DEVELOPMENT

The first semester my department asked me to teach a preprofessional writing course, I was fortunate to have a dialectical struggle going on just up the road from my university. A giant real estate developer, let us call it Kirsch and Associates, was attempting to win approval for zoning changes on a 1,500-acre parcel of land it had acquired several years before. In order to win approval for a larger proportion of office and retail space than had come with the parcel, which we can call "Winchester," Kirsch put together a "master plan." It was in the process of trying to sell the Winchester master plan to the three townships in which the land lay, when the semester began.

During the preceding summer, I had collected a number of articles from local papers on the progress of the master plan. On the first day of class, I divided the class into three groups and assigned each to research and write a position paper. Group A was to represent Winchester's interests; Group B represented the three local townships; Group C represented local environmental organizations. Each group had to interview its "constituency," gather as much information as possible, and share that information with the other groups.

In the course of their work, the groups stripped away much of the public relations rhetoric surrounding the Winchester master plan and uncovered the political maneuvering of the local governments and environmentalists. There were, the students discovered, two basic conflicts, one practical and one aesthetic.

Political opposition to Winchester in the affected local townships resulted from the additional traffic burden that rezoning the land promised to add to an already overcrowded suburban road system. The intersection of two extremely busy highways, "Northton Crossroads," lay at the southwest corner of the Winchester parcel, and the 1-million-square-foot mall, as well as the 7 million square feet of "office parks," promised to add anywhere from 40,000 to 80,000 vehicles per day to existing traffic.

The second point of contention concerned the aesthetics of development, the so-called open space movement. Winchester lay in the middle of an area of suburban sprawl, where the rural and agricultural character of the county was most obviously being transformed and, from the perspective of environmentalists and many who already owned homes there, "degraded." In short, two qualities that American culture values most found themselves in conflict with each other: economic development and rural (or exurban) simplicity.

Group A (representing Kirsch's interests) had a glossy brochure from which to begin its position paper. But the students immediately noticed that *Winchester: The Master Plan* was of little use in preparing its case. The language proved too vague to refute any of the charges that local citizens, township council members, and environmentalists made against the development project. Under "Transportation," for example, the brochure promised that the developer would construct a new interchange and connect it to existing roadways, and widen an existing road. It made no claims that these improvements would increase the carrying capacity of the roads by anywhere near the estimated 40,000–80,000 additional vehicles per day that development would add to local traffic. Instead, the Master Plan made generalizations: "Development brings changes, and a responsible developer will take measures to ensure a smooth transition. Consequently, a fundamental element of the *Master Plan* is the timely construction of the necessary roadways to support the development."

Meanwhile, Group B discovered that local township council meetings were boiling over with opposition to Winchester. Citizens were asking council members—many of whom had originally supported the development as a way to increase the local tax base—for specifics about increased traffic. The cry went up that strikes terror into every suburban commuter: "Gridlock!" Group B's position paper put it like this:

According to the best estimates of increased traffic through Northton Crossroads, the average time to get through the intersection during commuting hours will increase from 7 to 17 minutes. Delays at other intersections in the area will increase proportionally. Winchester will cost local commuters thirty minutes or more every day. This is one of the things Kirsch means when they say, "Development brings changes."

Group A (the Kirsch representatives) had pretty well anticipated the opposition to the traffic problem. They emphasized the incremental nature of the Winchester development: "The Master Plan calls for developing only about 100 acres a year over the next 15 years. This gradual development will allow time for the local traffic infrastructure to grow to meet demands. And Winchester will be contributing tax dollars to finance this growth."

Group C interviewed several local environmental groups that opposed the development. While there were numerous objections to the destruction of "open space" and to other fairly technical problems, including alleged damage to the area's aquifer, environmentalists had apparently chosen to focus on an embarrassing shortcoming in the master plan: inadequate means of sewage disposal. Winchester occupied a hillside and valley drained by only one fairly small creek. In winter, the creek froze over, leaving no way to discharge effluvia from the development. The need for individual septic systems was one reason the parcel had not already been subdivided.

In its brochure, Kirsch had glossed over the problem: "Various proposals are being considered to provide the necessary sewage service. Whatever is ultimately chosen, it will be implemented in strict accordance with all environmental regulations." Group A had interviewed Kirsch's civil engineering consultants and discovered that the most feasible plan for winter disposal set aside a thirty-acre strip stretching along the creek bank over which treated sewage would be sprayed while the creek was frozen up. Group C decided to make this plan (which, by agreement, Group A had to disclose to the rest of the class) central to its position paper.

As the position papers developed, it became increasingly clear that Kirsch was not going to get the Winchester parcel rezoned. Students were immersed in the politics of this conflict. Most came away from the assignment with a much clearer understanding of the politics of written discourse and specifically of the way business and professional writing (like all writing, in one way or another) is driven by the material interests of parties in dispute.

COMPANY POLICY ON WASTE DISPOSAL AND REDUCTION: A CASE STUDY

Another research group began with an idea of investigating the public relations department of a major chemical manufacturer, here given the pseudonym Ross Chemical. Ross has been embroiled recently in EPA investigations into alleged toxic waste emissions. The students wanted to examine the process by which Ross handled its public response to charges of pollution. Unable to interview any public relations contacts at Ross, the group shifted its focus to Ross's internal regulation of emissions.

The project began to take shape when one member of the "Ross group" obtained excerpts from a company operating manual,[1] what Freed and Broadhead call a "sacred text." This document was basically patterned on an enormous volume of EPA regulations. It combined specific operating rules ("Guidelines for Laboratory Sinks," for example) with more general statements of company policy ("Waste Reduction Policy and Plan"). In a conference with me, the group agreed to focus on the policy declarations of the corporate operating manual, evaluating them from a public relations and from an environmentalist perspective. Group members would focus on specific formulations that worked against presenting corporate policy in the best—most environmentally sensitive—light. The study would analyze, therefore, two sections of the manual that seemed to suggest poor corporate citizenship: "Policy on Controlling Air Emissions" and "Ross's Waste Reduction Goals." Later, the group presented these documents for class discussion as examples of the business writing process they were studying.

In their final case studies and group presentation, the students found statements of Ross's environmental policy insensitive to public concerns. To one student, the rhetoric "sounded as if the company really didn't think there was much danger to the environment." This is a serious lapse for a company that, according to its own operating manual, routinely disposes of "arsenic, chromium, lead, mercury, selenium, silver, zinc, and cyanide compounds" as well as "biocides and pesticides that persist in the environment."

In both their individual case-study research papers and their group presentation, the students attributed Ross's apparent lack of concern for the environment to the operating manual's rhetoric. Actually, Ross repeatedly insisted on its commitment to environmental safety. According to its "Waste Reduction Policy and Plan," Ross "is committed to an ongoing effort to minimize the environmental impact of our operations and . . . to minimization of all waste systems." But the students, taking their work on this project altogether, discovered three basic rhetorical failures in the manual excerpts that undermined the company's credibility as an environmentally conscious organization. Let me briefly summarize these failures under separate headings.

1. *The priority of profitability.* Ross's "Corporate Waste Reduction Goals" maintain that the company "will strive to continually reduce the generation of wastes consistent with maintaining our . . . economic competitive[ness]." Shortly after, this three-page document states that the "process for continual reduction of wastes will include a test of cost reasonableness and economic viability." On the next page, another short policy statement, "Policy on Controlling Air Emissions," warns employees that any discharge "noticeable outside our property line" could result in "harmful public relations, possible damage claims, and possible fines from governmental regulatory agencies." As one student put it,

"Concluding the introduction to a document that is supposedly dedicated to environmental safety with comments such as these is not conducive to its alleged purpose." Another wrote: "The company's legal liability seems to be more important throughout this document than environmental protection." All agreed that the company should not make environmental safety contingent on profit, as the operating manual repeatedly appears to do.

2. *The relativizing of commitments.* All group members noticed what they called "vague" or "safe" wording of the company's assurances about environmental protection. These assurances had, as discussed above, already been made dependent on bottom-line factors. They are further diminished by "weasel words." Ross announces, for example, that its "ultimate goal will be to eliminate any significant environmental impact of our wastes and if possible to eliminate waste streams altogether"; that its "high volume solvents" should be recycled "when practicable"; and that "small residual quantities of unused chemicals" should, *"where appropriate,* be placed in the reaction/formulation waste stream" (emphasis added). This wording in effect commits the company to little or nothing, but as the students noted, continual reiteration of well-hedged good intentions creates an impression of concern.

3. *The evacuation of responsibility.* All four participants in this group research project noticed that responsibility for operational safety traveled downward in Ross's hierarchy. One student wrote that "there is no mention or reference as to what person or agency decides what is 'significant' in a phrase like 'significant environmental impact.'" Another student pointed out the prevalence of passive verbs (e.g., "organic rinsings . . . should be disposed of properly"), which obscure the issue of who, in fact, is responsible for protecting the public and the environment from toxic wastes. Who, after all, is Ross Chemical, let alone "line management and the individuals who handle . . . undesirable gases or vapors" and whom the operating manual charges with responsibility for accidental emissions? When the manual turns to discussion of accidents endangering the environment and the public health, responsibility seems to reside, if anywhere, at the lowest echelon of the corporate hierarchy.

These characteristics of the text are all closely related, and to a Marxist perhaps too obvious for comment. The priority of "economic viability for the business" inevitably makes noncontractual commitments to the public's health and to environmental integrity relative indeed, and the commodification and alienation of labor ensure that work will be easily abstracted from serious responsibilities beyond the balance sheet.

While this diagnosis seems persuasive to me, it did not seem "practical" or "realistic" to my students when the class discussed the outcome of the research project. While we were all certainly worried about the risks posed by Ross's chemical waste stream (what I see as the conflict between cost/price competition and the public interest), class members judged them unavoidable, and therefore acceptable. And far from arriving at the radical outcome, the student researchers concluded only that Ross's interests were poorly served by its written discourse—as if improving the rhetoric might result in reducing the risk.

But the dialectical approach to business writing did teach students some things that they wouldn't have learned in a more traditional class. They learned, for one thing, that the so-called real world is far from being "above politics," once we understand that politics is about money and power and right and wrong. They also learned that the way we use language is political, shaping the reality of the world rather than reflecting it. It follows, therefore, that the discourse of Ross's operating manual deserves no claim to objectivity and common sense but merely serves the company's material interests.

Quite apart from issues of civic responsibility and political values, teaching preprofessional writing dialectically better prepares students for the corporate world most of them will inhabit. As another student investigation of writing in practice reveals,[2] discursive relations within the corporate infrastructure are often self-consciously adversarial. The group found that the technical writers in the research and development department of an international pharmaceutical company (XYZ Corporation) are specifically charged with resisting and refuting the "truth claims" advanced by the corporate marketing department. In one instance reported by the students, XYZ's marketing department wanted to introduce a swine feed additive, approved and marketed in Europe, into the United States. The company's R&D department was charged with the responsibility for "making the case" against marketing's claims for the product's efficacy and safety, claims the FDA would eventually hear before granting approval. R&D's role was that of a corporate watchdog, working to disconfirm the research presented in support of marketing's claims for the product. The role of XYZ's marketing department, according to one student, was "to try to hoodwink R&D, the FDA, and ultimately the consumer." In this case, however, R&D's version of the "facts" prevailed, and the plan to market the feed additive was scrapped.

At least occasionally, therefore, companies like XYZ consciously exploit the dialectics of contention to construct the most profitable or the most prudent truth.[3] While the formal surface of business and technical discourse may seem untroubled, conflicting claims are always circulating at one lower level or another. For this reason, a dialectical approach to business or technical writing, by insisting that students learn resistance as well as conformity to conventions, teaches them to be more inventive thinkers, more articulate writers, and perhaps even more conscientious citizens.

NOTES

1. All quotations from the operating manual come from photocopies of the excerpts that students turned in as appendices to their individual case studies. Field research at Ross Chemical was done by West Chester University students Charles Eberle, Rebecca Payes, Dana Pinner, and Renee Smith. In addition, the following students contributed to the critique of the operating manual and are quoted anonymously in this essay: Lea Asti, Karen Hagen, and Michelle Todd.

2. The students who investigated technical writing at XYZ Corporation are Diane Arcuicci, Christopher Kelly, and Beverly Kiefer.

3. On the institutionalization of conflict among technical writers, see Susan Wells.

Chapter 6

Science and Self-Expression: The Cognitive Turn in Historical Retrospect

With professional talk turning in recent years to social-epistemic theories of discourse and the institutional practice of writing—that is, to the *context* of composition—the time seems ripe to examine cognitive-process theory as a discourse situated within our recent professional history. What I mean by "cognitive-process theory" is the discursive practice of focusing theoretical attention on inferential models of what goes on in the black box of the mind while writing occurs.

At a recent annual meeting of the Conference on College Composition and Communication, a panelist went to considerable trouble to draw a distinction between what he called "context-specific" and "context-neutral" assignments. While it is a corollary of my argument here that there can be no such thing as context-neutral writing, since 1970 there has been a monumental attempt to formulate a theory of the writing process as a set of cognitive operations that might describe what goes on in the brain while written discourse is being produced. Stephen North calls this configuration of theoretical assumptions and research practices "cognitive formalism" to distinguish it from strictly empirical investigation, less strict clinical case studies, and ethnographic observation.

Cognitive formalism offers, in North's view, not a description of what happens in the world of empirical reality but instead an "abstract account of what happens in a mode [of ordinary language]" (253). The distinction between context and cognition has perhaps been drawn most dramatically by John Warnock. Warnock distinguishes between "writing" as the textual and contextual manifestations of scribal acts and "writing*" as "the least a machine or a person would have to be able to do" to perform recognizable writing (4). "Writing*" is the mental process that can be inferred from the written product, what happens "From Brain to Ballpoint," in Ross Winterowd's phrase.

The emergence of cognitivism in the 1970s must be understood, it seems to me, as an episode in the politics of knowledge and as a "discourse" in Foucault's sense of a set of "practices that systematically form the object of which they speak" (*Archaeology*, 49). The discursive formation of that object, "*the* composing process," was driven by the need for composition theorists and practitioners to "break out of the ghetto" and to "reach the status of a respectable intellectual discipline" (396), in Janice Lauer's words.

In the historical sketch that follows, I want to document the evolution of this effort to abstract the mental processes from the social and material context of writing and to identify it with traditional American ideology, which subsumes the process of cultural reproduction—which is inherently political—under the category of the natural—which is predetermined, amenable to scientific investigation, and thus inevitably outside the realm of politics. George Dillon has put the point most succinctly: "There is an ideology that attempts to ground social conventions and institutions, particularly existing ones, on biological realities: it is called Social Darwinism, and its chief architect was Herbert Spenser" (18).

Let me hazard a few observations about the historical conditions impelling the turn to a putatively scientific, cognitive model of the composing process. Looking back into the late 1960s, to the Dartmouth conference and its aftermath and to the more general emphasis on individual "consciousness" as a political concept, we can see the profound subjectivist or "expressionist" cast of American culture in general. In the early 1970s, these overt movements began to recede before the sobering economic realities of oil shortages, inflation, recession, and shrinking job opportunities for college graduates. For universities this meant declining enrollments and appropriations, which together with abolition of core requirements in the humanities, pressured English departments to make cutbacks beginning, naturally, with largely untenured composition faculty (Berlin, *Rhetoric*, 178–83).

In those years of retrenchment immediately preceding the discovery of the literacy "crisis" ("Why Johnny Can't Write," *Newsweek*, December 8, 1975), practitioners were driven to find new theoretical justifications for required composition instruction. The literacy crisis, often aggravated by open admissions policies, merely added fuel to already burning concerns to establish a more self-conscious rationale for studying and teaching writing. The perceived decline of writing ability seemed to demand something new, something that "worked," and in the best tradition of American pragmatism, that something needed to be scientific. Theoretically and pedagogically, expressionism was not working. Any new theory of composition would need to claim the prestige of science and thereby pass the increasingly conservative scrutiny of trustees and legislatures primarily concerned with business and economic conditions. These concerns, grafted onto the traditional American ideology of individualism, provided a perfect climate for the theoretical turn to cognitive science.

As an emerging set of discursive practices, the cognitive-process theory of composition grew out of the institutional requirements of those in English departments charged with teaching students to write. In the historical conditions of the 1970s, teachers, researchers, and theorists of writing were impelled to create a new object of study, one that not only explained the production of student texts but also allowed them to intervene pedagogically in the *process*. The result was, in Maxine Hairston's words, to focus study on "how people's minds work as they write" ("Winds of Change," 85).

There was, no doubt, a set of social imperatives at work in what contemporary observers called this "emerging paradigm." The cognitivist approach to the writing process was and is, as Berlin has charged, "compatible with the ideology of the meritocratic university" in that it privileges learning "to think in a way that will realize goals, not deliberate about their value" ("Rhetoric," 482–83). I want to emphasize here, however, three interrelated characteristics of the emerging cognitive discourse on the composing process, which together are historically embedded in the American tradition of pragmatism, our culture's dominant response to (and mechanism for avoidance of) social conflict.

The cognitive approach to the writing process is first of all *individualistic*. The composing activity is represented phenomenologically, the subjective mind's consciousness of materiality being abstracted from epistemic claims to describe or explain the world as it might in reality be. As Linda Flower puts it: "I use the problem-solving paradigm to help students observe their own thinking, to recognize their power as constructive thinkers, and to reflect on their goals, their strategies and their reading of the world around them" ("Comment," 766). Like self-expressionist rhetorics, therefore, cognitivism locates meaning in the individual mind's shaping of language. But the reverse process, by which language (and the material and cultural context of discourse) shapes individual subjectivity, is obviated.

A second, and closely related, characteristic of cognitive process theory is its *context-independence*, its determination to avoid social and political issues by concentrating instead on "control" of writing in the interest of private goal-oriented achievement and problem-solving (here, see Brooke and Dobrin). While problem-solving occurs in the mind, problems often occur in the world. Because public policy and social problems lie outside the mental domain of cognitive processes, writing can be severed from the material interests it advances in the world.

It was, however, the claim to a *scientific* order of certitude that made the cognitive approach to writing most attractive to a profession in crisis. Into an almost theoretically incoherent field of study, cognitivism introduced both a new model of the writing process and a new research methodology. Composing-aloud protocols and other behavioral research techniques allowed researchers to make hypotheses and test inferences about the operation of the mind *during* the composing process. For many, composition seemed about to ground its claim to authority in the culturally prestigious status of science.

DONALD MURRAY AND THE PROCESS OF
SELF-EXPLORATION

One point that has not been adequately appreciated is the theoretical continuity of cognitivism with the expressionist view of writing as a phenomenological process of self-creation. The idea that composing is primarily an individual search for meaning, separable from cultural practices and social interaction, was articulated most forcefully in the late 1960s by Donald Murray. For Murray, however, the writer was not merely a web of biocircuitry, traversed by thought and intention, but a unified, autonomous ego—romantically, heroically aloof from cultural and social formations—transfiguring the chaos of phenomena into a coherent text. In "The Explorers of Inner Space" (1969) and "The Interior View: One Writer's Philosophy of Composition" (1970), Murray represented the writing process as a tangible articulation of the interaction between the subject and the world. The act of writing offered the means for individuals to appropriate reality as "they discover what they have to say" ("Explorers," 3).

For Murray, the writer is an executive authority engaged in an autonomous process of discovering his or her own will. The metaphor of the executive is used explicitly: "The writer is a cold executive, making a thousand decisions in a paragraph, hiring one word, firing another" ("Explorers," 6). But writer-as-artist is a more frequent analogy. The writer uses language as a medium, "to lead him to understanding," in the same way other artists use other media to "realize" the phenomena of the world:

The painter doesn't paint colors he has seen, he uses color on the canvas to see. The composer uses the notes on the piano to hear. The writer doesn't write down words to photograph what is in his head, he uses words to set an experiment in motion. ("Interior View," 22)

The source of language, as of artistic vision, is in the head; the cultural and material world is contingent.

This romantic conception of composing is further reinforced by the fact that assertions about the writing process are almost always individuated: Murray writes of his own experience as a writer, or else he generalizes about "the writer" who is "lonely" before the blank page and who is engaged in the endless struggle of rendering order out of chaos:

[The writer] has learned to accept the mercurial conditions of discovery once he begins to write. . . . The writer, fearing change but accepting it, exists in a creative turbulence, tossed between the opposite tensions of creativity and control. . . . And the writer, obsessed with chaos, has a psychological need to tell himself stories, to find order in the universe symbolized through the artist's form. ("Explorers," 5–6)

Above all, however, in Murray's exposition of writing the decontextualized subject is the focal point of the process. The autonomous author is the source of truth: "writing is frankly personal," and it "is an individual search for meaning in life" ("Interior View," 21). The writer "must be self-centered" and unencumbered by history: "The writer uses the traditions which work for him, and he rejects the traditions which do not. . . ." The student writer is encouraged to take the "interior view" and to use writing to discover "meaning and understanding in his own experience" (22–25). Murray sums up his philosophy of composition in one proposition: "A writer is an individual who uses language to discover meaning in experience and communicate it" (21). The writing course, therefore, "should have one central purpose: to allow the student to use language to explore his world" (24).

JANET EMIG AND THE COMPOSING PROCESS

As influential as Murray's "interior view" of writing was (and continues to be), it was Janet Emig who translated self-expressionism into the quasi-scientific discourse of cognitive process. In his introduction to Emig's *Composing Processes*, Earl W. Buxton underscored the novelty of "an investigation of the writing *process*," which was "an area hitherto almost untouched by researchers in written composition who by and large have focused their attention upon the *written product*" (v). This focus, Buxton observed, was basically individualistic:

[A] question that has loomed large in most discussions of contemporary education . . . is what happens to the student's *self* as a result of the educational process. In essence, [Emig] is attempting to identify the student's feelings, attitudes, and self-concepts which form the invisible components of the "composition." (v)

The focal point of Emig's monograph, however, was its transformation of the student's text, as a product of the self, into an abstract simulacrum of verbal behavior during the composing process.

This transformation began with the invidious distinction between "extensive" or "school-sponsored" writing and "reflexive" or "self-sponsored" writing. The extensive mode of composing "focuses upon the writer's conveying a message or a communication to another"; its style is "impersonal and often reportorial" (4). This is the mode associated with writing about "abstract topics, such as the draft, drug addiction, and the ABM missile system" (92). It is worth remembering that the escalation of the Vietnam War, the Kent State shootings, and the bombing of Cambodia were occurring at the very time Emig was writing these words. Her ability to distance herself from these far-from-abstract conflicts attests to the "objective" researcher's inclination to ignore the sociopolitical context of discourse.

In contrast to the extensive mode, reflexive writing "focuses upon the writer's thoughts and feelings concerning his experiences; the chief audience is the writer himself; the domain explored is often the affective; the style is tentative, personal, and exploratory" (4). Reflexive writing, then largely absent from the high school curriculum (and thus necessarily "self-sponsored"), is almost identical to Murray's "interior view" that writing in school should "allow the student to use language to explore his world."

What has happened here is that public discourse and the traditional concerns of rhetoric have become associated with "sterile, mechanical production" of the (negatively valorized) product. Self-expression, on the other hand, has become a reflexive process, a mode of illumination through which students reformulate and transform an outer—and other—world of experience.

Emig's representation of her subject Lynn's composing process polarizes the reflexive and extensive modes of discourse. Extensive writing is associated with product, with "sending a message, a communication out into the world for the edification, the enlightenment and ultimately the evaluation of another." That other is most often "a teacher, interested chiefly in a product he can criticize rather than in a process he can help initiate through imagination and sustain through empathy and support" (97). Reflexive writing is thus associated with close interaction of student and teacher, the latter acting as midwife to the expression of the student's feelings about the world. This expressive process is, in Emig's formulation, clearly privileged over the product of discourse.

There is, however, a highly ironic outcome to Emig's bifurcation of product and process, for the subjects of her research—the actual "composing selves" of her text—vanish in the very process of their self-expression, leaving only the residue of their "products." The subjects of research disappear because Emig's methodology, the "composing aloud" protocols, transforms their self-expression into "composing behaviors and hesitation phenomena of various sorts" (41). In the pages of *Composing Processes* there is a decisive if subtle shift of attention from students writing texts to researchers "writing" protocols of "verbal behavior."

Whatever their relationship to the cognitive mechanics of the writing process (on this, see Cooper and Holzman), composing-aloud protocols provided data of a new order, a new stratum of texts that would become a "discourse" by which researchers constituted themselves as part of a legitimate field of investigation (Foucault, *Archaeology*, 46–49). In the decade following its publication, Emig's methodology rather than her concern to promote reflexive writing in the schools had by far the greater influence on composition studies. Research based on this textualization of the writing process seemed to offer the cultural legitimacy of a scientific endeavor, a generalizable account of discourse exclusively in terms of cognitive and linguistic performance. The protocols were more legitimate because they were produced by researchers, whose approach was "scientific" in that it was concerned only with observable, and thus context-independent, data. Researchers could excise the student both as a unique individual and as a subject of culture.

Thus Emig concluded a study of individual students' writing, a work advocating that teachers focus on the "private writing life" of students, with a call for a more abstract, impersonal methodology: "Perhaps the most promising aspect of this study for further research and model construction is the characterization of the behaviors involved in composing aloud" (*Composing Processes*, 96). In addition to continuing case-study protocols, the "most promising" methods require "finer calibration" and "cross-checking techniques and mechanisms" like time-lapse photography, an electric pen for recording hesitations in writing (an instrument developed by James Britton's research team at the University of London), and perhaps the "foot-shuttle-shutter" suggested by Richard Braddock (96–97). This technologizing of composition research severed writing from both the affective domain of the writer, about which Emig genuinely cared, and the social domain, about which she did not.

BIOLOGISM AND COMPOSITION

A second widely influential text in the theoretical turn to cognitivism was Lee Odell's 1973 essay "Piaget, Problem-Solving, and Freshman Composition." Odell, by presenting writing as a form of adaptive behavior, linked composition theory to a central subtext of American pragmatism: social Darwinism. As a rhetorical strategy, biologism aspires to evade social conflict by abstracting individuals out of culture and history and placing them in unmediated confrontation with exigencies of "natural" determination.

Odell argued that since writing improves "only as students grow intellectually, we shall have to understand and assist students with that growth. And to do so, we shall have to be familiar with recent work in the psychology of human development" (36). The model of "development" Odell adopts is Piaget's: the constant dialectic between a constitutionally quiescent subject and environmental disruptions of the subject's "equilibrium." The phenomenology of the individual's experience of the world is central to this adaptive process:

We try to alter our surroundings (people as well as objects) to suit out own needs and purposes; we select and shape experiences in accordance with the "structures"—i.e., the hopes, fears, memories, conceptual categories—that comprise our "internal world." Obviously, we can only do a certain amount of assimilating. At some point we have to modify these structures, make them "accommodate" the uniqueness and complexity of experience. (36)

The subject's perception of "dissonance" provides an impetus to adapt behavior to outside stimuli, to "accommodate." This process Odell termed "problem-solving," which he defined as

any situation in which an individual identifies some dissonance or disequilibrium and explores both the internal and external world in the hope of arriving at an insight or intuiting a hypothesis that will allow him to restore equilibrium. (37)

The object of behavior is to reduce conflict with "the world around us," that is, to establish equilibrium. Problems, in Odell's behavioral model of cognition, are inevitably personal and individual, and their solution results in a state of harmony that might be described as self-satisfaction.

Students' work in formulating problems from their reading in current events, for example, is designed to show

(1) that problems arise when an individual becomes aware of some dissonance and (2) that one's ability to solve a problem depends in large part upon his ability to explore and revise his internal world, to examine data thoroughly, and to reformulate the questions he poses. (40)

The implication is unmistakable: we solve problems by conforming to the outside world.

The aim of a composition course, according to Odell, should be the creative and effective solution of problems (i.e., resolving dissonance and achieving equilibrium):

[W]e ought to help students learn to identify as clearly as possible those areas of experience which cause some dissonance. If some of the activities in this process of achieving equilibrium are conscious and learnable, we ought to teach them; so far as we can, we ought to show students what strategies they use when they think and what they can do to think well. In short, we ought to teach students to formulate and solve problems as creatively and effectively as possible. (37)

For all its scientific rationale, however, Odell's pedagogy bespeaks traditional liberal humanism and is overtly self-expressive. Students are presented with literary works and assigned to write essays: "Formulate and solve what seems to you an interesting problem concerning the work you have read" (39). Readings in F. Scott Fitzgerald, Arthur Miller, Shirley Jackson, and Samuel Butler, supplemented by pictures, films, and a taped debate, become a pool of "problematic materials" (meaning situations capable of being cast as problems to be solved) from which student writers attempt "to formulate reasonable hypotheses" that lead them individually toward (re)solution.

Beneath the surface privileging of "problem-solving" lies Odell's premise that better writing requires "intellectual development." By analogizing the composing process to biological processes of development and adaptation, Odell's oft-cited essay opened the gates to the influx of behavioral theory—especially cognitive psychology—which has always treated language as a neutral medium by which individuals communicate with the outside world. The political implications of this position should be clear: the individual is encouraged to discover the means of adjustment to authority, those in a position to make "problems" for her or him. The process, in short, is conformity to the status quo, but of course this conformity is not represented as a *political* position. It is universal, in the nature of "all human development" (36). Students are encouraged to acquiesce in the flux of experience, instead of assuming an ethical responsibility for their relations with it.

LANGUAGE AS A FUNCTION OF MIND

The recent history of linguistics in this country, in particular the dominance of generative-transformational and structuralist "grammars," provides an instructive parallel to the emergence of the cognitive-process theory in the 1970s model of composition. In composition studies there has been the same search for an "autonomous" process of writing—and the consequent marginalization of humanistic and sociological approaches—that Frederick J. Newmeyer finds in linguistics. In both fields, the tendency has been to define the process of language performance strictly as a psychological phenomenon, usefully studied, therefore, as a developmental science (Newmeyer, 5–13).

And as in the so-called hard sciences, "autonomous" linguistics focuses on those attributes of language that can be abstracted from the cultural subjectivity and social interests of individuals who know a language. In other words, the cognitive model of composition abstracts "performance" from its cultural and social context in the same way that "grammars" have been divorced from their actual use in social life. Critics of cognitivism such as Patricia Bizzell and James Berlin echo Dell Hymes's charge that autonomous linguistics is "ideological" because it posits "an abstract and isolated individual, not, except contingently . . . a person in the social world" (quoted in Newmeyer, 53).

In his important "Problem-Solving" essay, Odell adopted, by way of Kenneth Pike, a concept of linguistic processing based on Jerome Bruner's studies in cognition. (On the earlier history of cognitive psychology's influence on rhetoric and composition studies, see Berlin, *Rhetoric*, 159–65). Problem-solving, Pike argues, first of all requires breaking experience down into "recallable, namable chunks" that can be clearly perceived only by contrast with all other "chunks" and by relative location in a larger scheme or system of categorization (Odell, 39). Odell does not explain in any detail how Pike's cognition-based linguistics might inform pedagogy; he seems more interested in establishing the composing process as an autonomous subject for scientific investigation. Intellection becomes a mechanical process: abstraction, reification, and manipulation of "discrete elements by our mental equipment" (Pike, quoted in Odell, 39). This phenomenological system encases language in individual minds, side-stepping any critique of a discourse's ideological interests by conceiving of writing in value-neutral linguistic terms.

It was also in the early 1970s that composition theorists, following Janice Lauer's admonition, began to introduce invention heuristics adopted from psychology and language science. In a 1973 essay, Ross Winterowd advocated a linguistics-based tripartite formula for invention at the propositional, the inter-propositional (syntactic), and the transi-tional (tagmemic) levels. He represented his "topics" as a "technical breakthrough" allowing students to "solve the problem implied by the question 'what can I say about this subject?'" (708). Although this heuristic is founded on the science of language, its purpose, according to Winterowd, is to provide a "means whereby the student can most efficiently gain the liberation that self-expression gives him" (708). Thus, technology will set our students free to pursue creative individual expression, outside the context of society with its ongoing struggle over inequalities of wealth and power. Like other grammatical and tagmemic heuristics, Winterowd's belongs to the wider search for a value-free, scientific theory of composition, one that would at the same time enhance the prestige of the field and enable the continued insulation of private experience from the politics of discourse.

LINDA FLOWER AND COGNITIVIST RHETORIC

In 1977 Linda Flower (most often in collaboration with John R. Hayes) began to publish a series of articles and books that have become the most thorough and elegant application of cognitive science to eluci-dation of the writing process. This work synthesized the various aspects of the brain-to-ballpoint process discussed above: the ethnomethodology of Janet Emig's *Composing Processes*, the behavioristic Piagetian struc-turalism of Lee Odell's problem-solving approach, and the interest in heuristics as formal techniques of composition exemplified by Winterowd's work. Taken together as *the* composing process, the cog-nitivism of Flower and Hayes sealed off—completely, in theory—the autonomous "composing self" from the social sources and cultural determinants of discourse.

In their 1977 essay "Problem-Solving Strategies and the Writing Process," the earliest of their publications in composition studies, Flower and Hayes present writing as a task originating somewhere outside the writer's mind and assumed under institutional aegis:

Within the classroom, "writing" appears to be a set of rules and models for the correct arrangement of preexistent ideas. In contrast, outside of school, in private life and the professions, writing is a highly goal-oriented, intellectual performance. It is both a strategic action and a thinking problem. ("Problem-Solving," 449)

The phrase "strategic action" in the context of writing assigned in schools and demanded by professional work implies the kind of adaptive behavior that Odell calls "achieving equilibrium" and that has become known as conforming to conventions of discourse. In any case, it is not action in the world that interests Flower and Hayes but composing as a "thinking problem."

They define writing as an "inner, intellectual *process*" and as an "array of mental procedures people use to process information in order to achieve their goals" (449–50). These procedures comprise the two basic "intellectual tasks" writers face: "(1) to generate ideas in language and then (2) to construct those ideas into a written structure" (452). The writer uses these mental procedures—heuristics—to "formalize" the methods of invention used by experienced writers. But these methods are entirely independent of the social "experience" and the experience of a cultural discourse, which are what make writers experienced in the first place. Thus, "ideas" said to be generated by individual application of heuristics are "original" (454).

Thus, by 1977, all the basic elements of an autonomous—that is, context-free—theory of the composing process were in place. Four years later, in the 1981 article titled "A Cognitive Process Theory of Writing," Flower and Hayes provide a more fully elaborated structural model of writing. In their well-known schematic diagram, the three basic functions are represented by boxes: at the center "Writing Processes"; above, "Task Environment"; to the side, "The Writer's Long-Term Memory." The interrelationship of the boxes—writing, task, and memory—is marked by reciprocating arrows, and subprocesses are indicated by smaller boxes nestled within the three macroprocess rectangles. With the publication of this model, it is safe to speak of the cognitive-process theory of composition as a fully elaborated discourse. By 1981, therefore, writing can be envisioned as a reified set of cognitive operations, free of any social or cultural context, except what might be present in the individual writer's long-term memory—"the raw material of experience," as Flower and Hayes put it in "The Cognition of Discovery" (21)—or in the "task" or "given" of the assignment.

For the purpose of their study, Flower and Hayes asked both novice writers and writing teachers, recipients of National Endowment for the Humanities (NEH) fellowships, to do the following assignment: "write about your job for the readers of *Seventeen* magazine, 13–14-year-old girls" (23). One may question the appropriateness of this assignment for inexperienced college writers, but even for most experienced teachers of writing, the "given" demands from the start that the writer abandon his or her ethos and social identity in order to perform the assignment. These "tasks" or "constraints," as Flower and Hayes call the exigencies of the assignment, require the writer to conform from the start to an editorial policy under which, as one subject of this study put it, women are looked at "as consumers of fashion and as consumers of men" (26).

There is no social world inside the confines of the assignment. Writing teachers might well have perceived their job as helping readers of *Seventeen* come to the realization that the magazine's management and stockholders were enriching themselves by instructing young girls in self-commodification. But the "given" nature of the problem, the notion of task and constraint, precludes a critical approach to this assignment. While each individual composes a unique text, according to Flower and Hayes, the composing process requires all to conform to the constraints of the assigned problem.

COGNITIVISM AND THE AUTONOMOUS SELF

The cognitive-process theory of composition, as I have sketched it above, beginning with Emig's "translation" of expressionism in *Composing Processes*, is situated in the American cultural tradition of pragmatic individualism. Emig charged, for example, that the exclusively unimodal writing in public schools (the extensive mode) was "other-directed" and "other-centered" (97). She has in mind here not only the current-traditional concerns with formal correctness of the written "product" (resulting in what she terms that "indigenously American" document, the five-paragraph theme), but also the equally American fear of encroachments on individual autonomy. While Emig does not cite David Reisman's *The Lonely Crowd*, her use of "other-directed" seems clearly to allude to that work.

Reisman identified three posttraditional relationships between the individual and his or her society: inner-directed, other-directed, and autonomous. The inner-directed personality is associated with the nineteenth-century capitalist ethos, while the other-directed is a "characterological adaptation" to bureaucratized, managerial society, requiring an individual sensitivity to peer-group expectations and norms (21–31). The hero of Reisman's triad, the autonomous character, is a modern fated to live among the other-directed, struggling to avoid determination by "the Kwakiutl-like institutions of America" and their "real and inevitable pressures for conformity" (286). Unlike the other-directed, the autonomous personality can escape "the process of socialization [that] fills up, crushes, or buries individuality" (286). This concern with insulating the individual from society and culture animates both Emig's endorsement of "self-sponsored," or "reflexive," writing and her deprecation of "extensive" writing—writing for communication with others.

Contemporary American signification of "self" carries with it heavy historical baggage. According to Peggy Rosenthal, the word entered early Modern English as a reflexive, and did not emerge as a noun until the Renaissance, when "reflexiveness became a subject" (11). Developing most of its denotative meaning in the seventeenth and eighteenth centuries, "self" took on its modern connotation during the Romantic era. American Romanticism in particular hypostatized the self, making it a metaphysical repository of divinity. In Emerson, the individual comes to represent the "divine idea," and as he puts it in "Self-Reliance": "No law can be sacred to me but that of my nature"; Whitman's "self" is even more imperial: "Nothing, not God, is greater to one than one's self is" (quoted in Rosenthal, 17).

In the twentieth century, post-Freudian psychology has secularized these effusions in the process of constructing a science of mind. The self becomes not only organic consciousness, the perceiving subject of experience requisite to an empirical age, but also an object or aim of therapeutic development, of personal growth. The consequent ideal of autonomy is exemplified in Rollo May's assertion that the "struggle to become a person takes place within the person himself." And the individual self is, according to a modern psychiatric reference work,

basically constructive, accepting, creative, spontaneous, open to experience, self-aware, and self-realizing. It is parental, societal, and cultural controls, through manipulation of rewards and punishment, which inhabit the otherwise natural development of self-expression and self-actualization. (quoted in Rosenthal, 28)

This intellectual climate and historical context out of which Emig's concept of the composing process emerged are discussed specifically and at some length in her 1980 essay "The Tacit Tradition." Within a decade after the publication of *Composing Processes*, Emig the critic at the disciplinary margin has metamorphosed into Emig the authority. She writes, by 1980, of composition as "our field" with its own "tacit tradition" or "set of authorities" through whom "[w]e view the universe" (146–48).

Emig's version of the emerging disciplinary orthodoxy in composition studies begins with Thomas Kuhn's definition of scientific revolutions as largely autonomous paradigm changes. But while Kuhn's emphasis is on the institutional construction of paradigm formation, elaboration, crisis, and shift, Emig is more interested in the individual, phenomenological interaction with the "world." She quotes Howard Gruber (a Piaget scholar and biographer of Darwin) approvingly: "When we think new thoughts we really are changing our relations with the world around us, including our social moorings" (148).

In a sentence like this, with the "we" able, apparently, to change its relationship to reality (and even break loose from "social moorings"), individuals have seized control of cultural formations and overthrown subjectivity. The "new thoughts" seem to come from the individual's independent transaction with the world that Kuhn believes is, in actuality, the creation of a knowledge community. Emig understands "the psychology of creative individual thought" as an essence that exists outside history, unmediated by the culture each individual human being inevitably must learn. (Bizzell, Robert Connors, and others have pointed out the misuse of Kuhn in "foundational" accounts of individual cognition or creativity.)

In any account of human communication, no matter how individualistic, there must be some opening to community, whether as audience, decoder, interpretive convention, or the like. For cognitivism, the "reality principle" of communication has been the schema, a Piagetian concept. The schema is essentially a cognitive wiring diagram (not unlike Chomsky's notion of linguistic rationality) predisposing individuals to communicable representations of the object-world, unmediated by culture.

In her "Tacit Tradition" of composition theory, Emig draws from a number of sources to place the cognitivist "paradigm" in a larger, cross-disciplinary context. Her "ancestors" include George Kelly, whose "Personal Construct Theory" proposes that linguistic processes "are psychologically channelized" by events and experience. From Susanne Langer, Emig borrows "symbolization" to explain the process by which the brain represents the object-world to itself and in so doing becomes "mind." This process, which she associates with Louise Rosenblatt's transactional theory of reading, is given a distinctly biological cast. A transaction is part of an ongoing process by which "the organism selects out and seeks to organize according to already acquired habits, assumptions, and expectations [from] the environment" (149–51). These thinkers—as well as Piaget, Vygotsky, Luria, Eric Lenneberg, and others—become Emig's fellow transactionalists in the tacit tradition of composition studies.

Biological science is the foundation of this tradition, Emig concludes:

If our criterion is explanatory power, and if the phenomenon of the brain's transformation to mind via the processes of symbolization is to be explained, I do not see how we can choose otherwise. If we agree that selected subprocesses orchestrate to produce writing, I also do not see that we can choose otherwise, since these subprocesses are all brain-based. (153–53)

With writing reduced to a group of biological subprocesses by which individual brains transform experiential data into personal meaning, the influence of culture and society is theoretically excluded. Emig affirms that individuals are "programmed to write, as well as speak" (153). The "program" (a term suggesting the influence of information science on cognitivism) is neurological, not cultural, a product of cognitive structures, not of the internalized social phenomenon—the Kuhnian paradigm—with which the argument began.

Emig writes of a "cognitive history of the twentieth century whereby literature and philosophy transform into psychology which in turn becomes, at times, biology" (155). In the domain of the human sciences, the cognitivist theory of the composing process is limited exclusively to the behaviorist, clinical, biological wing. The theory of writing is thus cleanly separated from cultural studies, from the history of social and material formations, from anthropology with its ethnomethodological study of cultures as textual activities, from literary and critical theory that explores that textuality as a political and rhetorical process. Composing is located in the individual circuitry of the mind.

THE RISE AND DECLINE OF COGNITIVIST-PROCESS THEORY

From the perspective of the foregoing analysis of cognitivist theory and practice, a historical sketch of composition studies since the late 1960s would begin with the high tide of self-expressionism that followed the Dartmouth Conference in 1967. I have represented that period with the writings of Donald Murray. Expressionism began to ebb in the early 1970s at the same time that Janet Emig's *Composing Processes* began to exert its influence. As I have argued here, Emig's slim monograph provided an intellectual and methodological bridge between expressionism and cognitivism by linking case studies of individual students' self-expression to a protoscientific system of gathering data—composing-aloud protocols—on which to base inferences about what was actually occurring in the minds of student writers.

A further step away from the subjectivism of the late 1960s, and toward a cognitivist theory of the composing process, was the transformation of procedures for invention (or "discovery," as it was most often called) into formal heuristics for "problem-solving." While Kenneth Pike, Janice Lauer, and Richard Larson, among others, had actually introduced generative procedures into composition studies, I have emphasized the more directly influential 1973 papers of Ross Winterowd and Lee Odell. Finally, I have presented the work of Linda Flower and John R. Hayes, which began to appear in 1977, as the culmination of the cognitivist-process theory of composition.

What has been obscured by this progressive overview is the state of theoretical incoherence that obtained in the professional literature until the late 1970s, when cognitivism came to be seen by many as a revolutionary new "paradigm" (Hairston) for studying and teaching writing. Let me give as an example of this intellectual diffusion a brief account of Emig's influence on composition research. In the National Council of Teachers of English's (NCTE) *Research in the Teaching of English (RTE)*, most of the studies reported were text-based linguistic analyses of student writing well into the 1970s. In fact, *RTE*'s did not even review Emig's *Composing Processes*, although as the years went by, the work reported in its pages increasingly adopted Emig's ethnographic methodology as recorded in composing-aloud protocols.

As early as 1973, Dwight L. Burton, in an analysis of contemporary research, referred to *Composing Processes* as "[p]erhaps the most significant recent study of the composing process" (178); and the following year Terry Mischel specifically applied Emig's method in "A Case Study of a Twelfth-Grade Writer." In 1975, Donald Graves's article, "An Examination of the Writing Processes of Seven Year Old Children," singled out Emig's as one of only two studies that "involved the actual operation of the behaviors of writers while they are in the process of writing" (227).

Graves's article is significant as evidence of the evolution of process theory because it is the first that distinguishes between "writing and the writing process" (241), thus confirming the existence of a new cognitivist "discourse," in Foucault's sense. With Graves's publication, we can be sure that the composing process has become an institutionalized discursive practice.

The years following 1975 saw a burgeoning of Emig's influence in research on composing. In *RTE*, volume 9 (1975), the Graves study was the only one of five articles indexed as studies of composition that employed ethnographic investigation of the composing process. By 1978, two of eight articles were case studies of the composing process (both cited Emig); in 1981, three of nine were (two of the three citing Emig); and in 1984, seven of ten articles reported ethnographic research. In this latter year, only three of the seven authors cited Emig. By 1984, however, researchers were referencing their work to that of Nancy Sommers, Sondra Perl, and others who had drawn on Emig's theory and method directly. The surest sign of influence, a substantial and clearly documented intertext, was already extant.

The theme of the Conference on College Composition and Communication in 1980 was "Writing: The Person and the Process," a title that could well have served Emig for her 1971 study. The growing influence of cognitivism in the conference can be traced by the number of papers referring to "*the* writing (or composing) process" in their titles. After 1973, in which there was only one (presented by Janet Emig), the numbers grew geometrically until the 1980 meeting.

The conference theme of that year encapsulates the historical influence of cognitivism on the study of writing as a disciplinary activity: the study and teaching of writing focuses on the *person* in the phenomenological *process* of transforming experience into expression. Of course, much good has accrued from this approach to writing. It opened a space for revision and for teachers to intervene, to teach students how they might elaborate and refine a piece of writing. It suggested, as well, the opportunity for a new and more democratic student-teacher dialogue, transforming composition instructors from mere guardians of literacy into counselors—in some cases even colleagues.

But cognitivism has had some less salutary effects as well. First, it reaffirmed the traditional American emphasis on the individual as a self-sufficient, autonomous agent of experience, an authentic self like Emerson's "Man Thinking." The effect, if not the motive, has been profoundly conservative, encouraging a conformist and careerist rhetorical posture that, as Berlin has warned, prepares students for uncritical service to institutional hierarchies. Second, cognitivism introduced a research method that further decontextualized writing by translating it into a record of internal mental processing. Composing-aloud protocols—student writing without the student—provided generalizable data, objects that could be subjected to the rigors of cognitive science. This new discourse created a value-free object of study at the cost of depoliticizing writing, or "refusing the ideological question," in Berlin's words ("Rhetoric," 482). The result has led away from the interface between individual and culture, from discourse as social dialogue, and from writing as an intertextual and cultural process.

Recent work by Linda Flower, Stuart Greene, and other proponents of cognitive formalism has attempted to incorporate "context" into models of the composing process. Although Flower, for example, writes of a "dialectic between cognition and context" ("Cognition," 286), the latter term always refers to environmental factors *outside* the mind of the individual writer—never to constituents of the writer's self-consciousness: "cultural and social context can provide direct *cues* to . . . and [is] always *mediated* by the cognition of the individual writer" (287). Cognition, in this scheme, is the process by which an essentialized composing self deals with the outside world. By contrast, most disciplines comprising the human sciences place "context" *inside* the individual mind. Instead of an autonomous *self*, contemporary theory posits a linguistically or discursively constituted *subject* of culture.

In Flower's assertion that "Cognition Mediates Context" ("Cognition," 289), we can glimpse the ghost in the machine: the metaphysical residue of the composing self, which was the central presumption of expressionist rhetorics like Donald Murray's. If cognition *mediates*—if it occupies a central position between two entities—what or who, besides context, is the other principle of the process? It is, I would suggest, the same autonomous, self-constituted ego—untouched by cultural and social formations—that Donald Murray called "explorers of inner space." I would conclude, then, with what would seem a more promising theoretical formula for the future: *Culture mediates cognition and context.*

It has been the central purpose of this chapter to account for the development of the cognitive-process theory of composition: the conception of individuated writers, each with his or her "own" ideas, who approach the composing process and language in general as a formal system by which they can set goals, represent tasks, conform to constraints, and ultimately achieve intended results. In recent years, there has been an increasing interest in what has come to be called the social, or epistemic, turn in composition studies. Berlin, Bizzell, and Greg Meyers, among others, have taught us that cognitivist rhetoric isolates writing from the political realities of live forums, obscuring the way discourses strain to reproduce extant distributions of social power by dressing rhetorical claims in the garb of knowledge. The eclipse of cognitivism is perhaps a recognition that writing belongs to a larger social process, one that occurs outside of and between individual minds and reproduces cultural forms as knowledge and social structures as power.

Chapter 7

Pragmatism, Politics, and Social Epistemology in Composition Studies

It is customary to characterize our age as one of major intellectual transformation, a time witnessing the dissolution of the belief that "truth" (positive knowledge) is a property of those—and only those—propositions that can be tested empirically. The old world of logical positivism was inhabited by solid objects in mathematical relationships to each other, which the human subject could make present—call up out of nature—by speaking their names. Through the instrumentality of language, the mind was, in Richard Rorty's phrase, the mirror of nature.

It was this (basically Cartesian) understanding of language that lay behind the strictures of current-traditional rhetoric. If words were just used "correctly," proponents of this view of communication admonished, then a writer's product might reflect a "reality" equally manifest to all reasonable speakers of a language and, through translations, to all humankind. Residues of this faith appear in our exhortation to precision in word choice. Thus, in the *Harbrace College Handbook*, Section 20: "Exactness," the writer is instructed to select "the exact word needed to express your idea . . . [the word] that precisely denotes what you have in mind" (247).

The implication of this dictum, that ideas can exist in the mind apart from language (as reflections of "reality"), is no longer tenable. There is no object or relation "outside" in nature that a subject merely perceives and matches "precisely" to a word that other subjects can likewise match with their own cognitive relations of the object-world. Language is primary; the world is contingent.

The collapse of this system whereby language names truths or realities independently existing in nature is most often associated, at least in rhetoric and composition studies, with Thomas Kuhn's *The Structure of Scientific Revolutions*. Kuhn's argument has been taken to mean that reality—even that mathematical reality of the so-called hard sciences—is not merely represented or reflected by sign systems (including mathematics) but is instead socially constructed in language. In spite of Kuhn's influence, however, the proposition that knowledge is constructed rhetorically by "communities" and not privately by individual mental processes, whether conceived of as cognitive or vitalist, has only recently begun to emerge as a governing conception of composition theory.

The "linguistic turn" in philosophy has created increasing anxiety in the various disciplinary knowledge communities, especially those that cling to a rhetorically innocent faith in the transcendent objectivity of their facts and logics. Much of this anxiety has been generated from within disciplines by critical practitioners like James Clifford in anthropology, Hayden White in history, Evelyn Fox Keller in biology, and Donna Haraway in primatology and paleoanthropology. Other rhetorical critics of disciplinary "dialects" of knowledge are located in English and communication departments. Taken together, the critique of scholarly discourses has begun to challenge the epistemic foundations of disciplinary knowledge by dissolving the distinction between inquiry and advocacy, truth and power, facts and values, knowledge and politics. This "rhetorical turn" in scholarship (Simons) or "rhetoric of inquiry" (Nelson et al.) marks the textual inlet of Kuhnian influence in introductory writing courses.

Much recent controversy about composition theory might profitably be viewed as an ideological tug-of-war in which the right attempts to snatch Kuhn's thesis away from the profession's left. The process began as early as 1978, when at the annual Conference on College Composition and Communication (CCCC) Maxine Hairston appropriated Kuhn's notion of "paradigm change" to advocate a theoretical shift of emphasis from the aesthetics (or at least the proprieties) of a student's written product to the empirical study of a student's cognitive processes while writing. Patricia Bizzell responded in an essay the following year, charging Hairston (and others, including Janet Emig) with "scientism" for her "appeal to empirical evidence . . . to establish a paradigm above the debate" ("Thomas Kuhn," 764). Bizzell argued that the paradigm stipulated the methodology and not the other way around:

[I]t is Kuhn's most striking point that a paradigm determines the identification and interpretation of "empirical evidence" in a given discipline. . . . [A] paradigm is established, even in the natural sciences, not because of compelling empirical evidence, but because of a rhetorical process that delimits the shared language of the intellectual community governed by the paradigm. (764)

Rather than indicating an empirical approach to studying composition, Bizzell maintained, the implications of Kuhn's argument pointed in the direction of the "social and historical" influence on knowledge, "the study of language as social product and embodiment of ideology" (768). The exchange between Hairston and Bizzell set in process the ongoing dispute between cognitivist individualism (whose most formidable contemporary proponent has been Linda Flower) and its leftist critics, most decisively James Berlin. Flower focused on the composing act in some abstract or hypothetical relationship to social and ideological forces—"the mediation of cognition by context," as she put it—while leftists saw writing as mediated not by a hypothetical context but by a specific set of social and historical imperatives that serve to reproduce existing inequalities of wealth and power. In 1988, Berlin defined a "social-epistemic rhetoric" that makes writing a "dialectical interaction of the observer, the discourse community (social group), in which the observer is functioning, and material conditions of existence." And, he insisted, "our notions of the observing self, the communities in which the self functions, and the very structures of the material world are all social constructions" ("Rhetoric," 488). Finally, practitioners of social-epistemic rhetoric were said to share "a notion of rhetoric as a political act," bringing to the composition classroom "both a detailed analysis of dehumanizing social experience and a self-critical and overtly historicized alternative [to cognitivist and expressionist rhetorics] based on democratic practices" (488).

In its actual pedagogical application, however, epistemic theory seems to have had very nearly opposite effects. While I share Berlin's hope that a post-Kuhnian theory of knowledge might yet make a genuinely critical rhetoric (i.e., a "materialist" rhetoric as I define it in chapter 2), epistemic theory seems to have been captured by very different political interests. Instead of enlarging the place of criticism in writing instruction, social constructionist discourse theory has more often authorized unreflective conformity to institutional discourse practices. So-called practical writing courses proliferate. Students are taught the conventions or forms of writing in various "disciplines"; they learn that writing advances private interests, that it is a marketable commodity that they can sell to employers in the growth industry of producing, storing, or marketing knowledge.

A genuine commitment to rhetoric, however, impels practitioners to interrogate this kind of formalism, to critique the reification of a discourse. I believe this is so because those practiced in rhetorical analysis can almost always perceive formular discourse as "rhetoric," and therefore as bad rhetoric. Of course, the reproduction of knowledge requires that students learn the conventions of institutional communication. This is a primary objective of the "research paper course"—very often the second-semester composition course that serves as an introduction to academic discourse(s).

Most writing instructors, however, want their students to develop a full repertoire: the means of cooperating and collaborating, to be sure, but the means as well of resisting, reversing, and restructuring truth claims. No program of formalist techniques will help our students locate themselves in a poststructural discursive world created by a cacophony of claims to knowledge. In our post-Kuhnian world, any proposition is unstable, at best a momentary consensus in the flux of language and history. The construction of knowledge is in this sense always political, always an argument for advancing, defending, or disputing a claim to represent reality. In this economy of knowledge, to deny the essentially interested nature of discourse is itself to assert a brazenly political proposition.

The rest of this chapter will concern itself with the struggle to break down the institutional and intellectual barriers that history has erected between knowledge and value. First, I will examine the historical appropriation—and the ideological containment—of social constructionism in composition theory and pedagogy. Second, I will use a contrastive analysis of two arguments in order to illustrate how social constructionism can serve to insulate institutional discourses from critique. (The succeeding chapter will offer an extended account of an academic writing course that introduces students to politics of knowledge formation.)

CRITIQUE AND CONFORMITY IN
SOCIAL-EPISTEMIC THEORY

One of the most influential arguments for a genuinely social-epistemic rhetoric was Patricia Bizzell's 1982 essay "Cognition, Convention, and Certainty." In this study, Bizzell acknowledged the cognitive factors in language use, what she called the "inner-directed" aspect, but she focused attention on the relatively neglected "outer-directed" elements of discourse, what she called "the social processes whereby language-learning and thinking capacities are shaped and used in particular communities" (215).

Outer-directed theorists, Bizzell writes, start by assuming that social conventions of language performance are part of language-learning.

Learning to think in language is thus local and not universal, as cognitivists (and structural linguists) conceive it. Acquiring a native language is equivalent to "learning traditional, shared ways of understanding experience" or the conventions of one's discourse community. We cannot separate language from discourse conventions because a "discourse gives meaning to words and not vice versa" (225). Our sense of the real, while a social construction, is mediated by culture and history.

Interpretive conventions, a term synthesized from Kuhn, Stanley Fish, and sociolinguistic theorists, grow out of a community's material relationships, according to Bizzell, and reflect its historical experience. In her memorable phrase, "knowledge is what language makes of experience" (223). By rooting the interpretive conventions of discourse communities in the conflicting interests of the material world, Bizzell's version of epistemic theory makes a place for rhetorical dissensus. Once we abandon the claim that writing—and the study of writing—can be understood as positivistic mimesis, as we must if we follow Kuhn's rejection of theoretical certainty, the process of establishing credibility is returned to public forums, where argument and persuasion decide what is to be accepted as knowledge by interpretive communities.

Bizzell insists that we must teach students to recognize the discourse conventions operative in multiple interpretive communities. She is emphatic, however, in her insistence that discourse analysis must include the study of cultural politics—the clash of competing claims to truth: "Otherwise, we risk burying ethical and political questions under supposedly neutral pedagogical technique" (213). The epistemological dispute over truth claims and over their ethical evaluation makes rhetoric "the central discipline of human intellectual endeavor" (239).

In the mid-1980s, however, epistemic discourse theory took a radically different direction from the one Bizzell projected. This divergence is most closely associated with Kenneth Bruffee's version of social constructionism. Bruffee's version, which we will now examine in some detail, has become the dominant strain of social epistemology in composition studies. His pragmatic, or what I will characterize as "particularistic," version of epistemic discourse theory authorizes (in my view) an apolitical and uncritical understanding of written discourse production. His particularism, by divorcing the construction of knowledge from history and from the ongoing social reproduction of culture (the site of rhetoric), conceals from our students the political nature of discourse and in particular the role of dispute and dissensus in the production of knowledge (see Sloane).

One should begin by remarking that Bruffee and Bizzell share much common ground, at least in their insistence that social context, not objective reality or cognitive processes, is the basis of language. Learning to write is thus better figured as social interaction than as self-expression. And collaborative learning, Bruffee's application of epistemic theory to pedagogical practice, parallels Bizzell's aversion to teaching local conventions as transcendent norms. As John Trimbur has pointed out, Bruffee's work has helped "reorganize the social relations in the classroom" by decentering the teacher as enforcer of authorized knowledge ("Consensus," 605). While this decentering of teacherly authority *may* serve as a prelude to critiquing disciplinary authority, it need not.

Trimbur calls our attention to the utopian possibiliites that collaborative learning offers for the cultivation of dissent: critical reading practices in literature classes. For composition instructors, the concern is with enabling dissensus by means of ethical argument historically situated in cultural texts. We need to avoid blurring the student's ability to distinguish between the ideal and the material worlds. Both are necessary: utopias are imaginary material realizations of an indealized social morality embedded in a culture's historical intertext. "Idealized social morality" is of course a contested term. And left to their own devices, students are most likely to idealize the material possibilities they are most familiar with: the images of commodity consumption (re)presented in the popular media.

The issue I am particularly interested in here is the textual sources—the historical transmission—of dissent. To enable what Trimbur calls dissensus, we need to do more than change our students' attitudes toward authority (essential though that be). We need to change their attitudes toward authoritative knowledge. To accomplish this, students will have to learn a critical practice that will problematize discursive conventions by subjecting them to ethical arguments historically situated in our culture's texts.

To return to Bruffee's influence on the appropriation of social constructionism by composition studies, I am concerned that his primary emphasis on collaborative learning has actually worked to undermine the individual's rhetorical resources for dissent and at the same time to authorize institutional preemption of the definition of knowledge. To practice Bruffee's version of social constructionism, in other words, is to enable students to conform to the "practical" conventions of writing that their future employers value most, while depriving them of the primary rhetorical strategy for constructing critical evaluation of "knowledge": ethos.

Ethical arguments are seldom as practical as expedient ones. They most often measure "results" or consequences not in terms of quantity or efficiency or rationality, but in terms of right and wrong. As Chaim Perelman explains in his small masterpiece, *Justice*, the burden of evidence always rests on proponents of change. Because arguments for change must appeal to cultural ideals of justice—must use ethos, that is—pragmatism, by its insistence on measuring a course of action by "results," devalues ethical arguments. It attempts to define a course of action above politics, one it defines as practical, as opposed to the "mere theory" of ethically valued alternatives.

Knowledge, according to Bruffee, is the result of negotiation "to justify belief to the satisfaction of other people within the author's community of knowledgeable peers" ("Collaborative Learning," 643). He called this negotiation "normal discourse," borrowing the term (via Rorty) from Kuhn's "normal science," the day-to-day work of paradigm elaboration, and broadening its application from disciplines of inquiry in the natural sciences to "academic, professional, and business communities." Normal discourse, which "in written form is central to a college curriculum" (643), constructs knowledge "by justifying it socially, that is, by arriving at a sort of consensus" ("Social Construction" 779). Learning, therefore, means learning to conform to discourse conventions that taken together constitute knowledge: "Knowledge is identical with the symbol system (i.e., language) in which it is formulated" (779).

There are two controlling concepts in this formulation that in effect insulate writing from its concrete social referent and its situation in history: "language" and "community." Each term deserves close scrutiny because each has worked to obscure the politics of knowledge in composition studies.

Bruffee's equation of knowledge with "language," as an abstract grammatical system, precludes a complete range of rhetorical practices (particularly Trimbur's dissensus) by failing to account for the role of ideological interests in the constitution of claims about reality. To resort to Terry Eagleton's aphorism, "without particular interests we would have no knowledge at all, because we would not see the point of bothering to get to know anything" (14). In literary theory, structuralism has served the purpose of separating formal characteristics of texts from social contexts in which they were written (and are read). Bruffee's pragmatic "antifoundationalism" performs a similar function for his theory of discourse. His analogue for discourse comes (via Rorty) from Michael Oakeshott's 1959 essay "The Conversation of Mankind."

This unending conversation was "begun in the primeval forests" (where conservatives are fond of locating contested practices), and its perpetuation is, according to Oakeshott, the real aim of education:

Education, properly speaking, is an initiation into the skill and partnership of this conversation in which we learn to recognize the voices, to distinguish the proper occasions of utterance, and in which we acquire the intellectual and moral habits appropriate to conversation. (quoted in Bruffee, "Collaborative Learning," 638–39)

The conversation metaphor—and its primarily oral representation of language—excludes dissensus in two ways. First, it disguises the unequal distribution of literacy. If writing is just "internalized social talk made public and social again" (641), the outcome of an open-access conversation, then it is fair to assume that conventions represent a genuine consensus. But as composition teachers know too well, the ability to read and write texts—the real currency of discourse communities—is not accurately signified by "social talk." To conflate speech, a universal human attribute, with competence in reading and writing obscures the fundamental hierarchy of social class and educational opportunity.

Second, the conversation metaphor disguises not only who may speak but also what may be spoken. Knowledge as a "consensus" constructed for the time being in language (641) is a synchronic system independent of the social and material realities to which people attempt to refer. There is no purchase for resistance to orthodoxies. But as Bruffee clearly understands, a completely conventionalist theory of discourse would lead to total entropy (646). We would finally agree on everything, losing the reason (in Eagleton's phrase) to bother with knowing anything.

To avoid this theoretical impasse reached by excluding dissensus, Bruffee borrows Rorty's notion of "abnormal discourse" (from Kuhn's "abnormal science"). Bruffee writes that normal discourse, "since it maintains knowledge . . . , is inadequate for generating new knowledge" (646) and that abnormal discourse "challenges" community authority and must "undermine" the conventional rhetoric of normal discourse, precipitating "crises of identity and authority" (648–49). How this might be done is unclear: normal discourse and its pedagogical equivalent, collaborative learning, are not usually said to be "an adversarial activity" (645), and joining knowledge communities is said to be accomplished "through assenting to those communities' interests, values, language, and paradigms of perception and thought" (646). There is not much play here for rhetorical dissensus.

What is missing in Bruffee's concept of discourse—and its theoretical descendants—is the idea of the text, the recognizable patterns of signification that shape the abstract potential of *langue* into *parole*. This failure to distinguish between the synchronic and diachronic phases of language has permitted social constructionists to avoid the clash of political interests by representing epistemic formations as coalescing independent of historical forces—in other words, of placing epistemology beyond ideology. Like the American pragmatic tradition out of which it grew, Bruffee's theory apologized for the status quo by denying its own engagement in cultural politics.

In fact, the concept of culture as inscribed in texts is practically absent from Bruffee's theory of discourse. In the place of specific discursive formations of culture, there is the abstraction "community." Thus, for example, instead of describing the individual self as a construct of culture, Bruffee writes that the self "is a construct largely community generated and community maintained" ("Social Construction," 777). This refusal to confront the cultural text and the political interests inscribed therein by invoking epistemological relativism of autonomous institutional "language" has unfortunately been the most influential aspect of Bruffee's social constructionism.

Joseph Harris has taken epistemic discourse theory to task for the vagueness of its foundational trope, "community," calling the term "a shadowy network of citations and references" abstracted from "social and material relations" (14–15). This terminological vacuity has been an ongoing problem in composition theory. At different times, Bruffee used "community" to refer to groups as different as canoeing enthusiasts ("Collaborative Learning," 644); members of academic disciplines, businessmen, and professionals; and everybody in the world (647–50). Which communities, teachers of composition might well ask, should exert the primary influence on writing pedagogy? Bruffee's answer seemed unambiguous: the conventional discourse that "we teach today—or should be teaching—in composition courses is the normal discourse of most academic, professional, and business communities" (643).

While we will be examining the discursive constitution of some business and professional communities more closely in a moment, for now we should note that Bruffee's formulation ignores ideology, that pervasive influence of social and material interests that makes conventions seems natural and inevitable. Although we may speak of a corporation as a "community," employers (owners and their representatives, managers) and employees have different interests, most would concede. Knowledge is not value-free; it serves material ends. As Greg Myers has put it in his critique of Bruffee's "knowledge community," the "knowledge of an accountant and knowledge of employees in a factory to be closed . . . cannot be resolved into a consensus without one side losing something"

("Reality," 167). The decision to teach students that writing is equivalent to conforming to the discursive conventions of corporate employers is a political, not merely an abstractly epistemological, one.

Nowhere are the politics more obvious than in Bruffee's claim that knowledge communities are composed of "status equals: peers" ("Collaborative Learning," 643). It is a commonplace of sociology that complex communities are hierarchical. Certainly in a society dominated by technologically sophisticated bureaucracies, we can speak of communities of peers only in the loosest terms. Even in the academic profession of English—a comparatively egalitarian knowledge community—status, power, and emoluments are highly stratified. And all, from the full professor of literature to the itinerant part-time composition instructor, are subordinate to politically sensitive administrations in our college and university communities. As I hope the following section makes clear, teaching students that knowledge makes them in any real sense peers in corporate hierarchies is a political mystification that obscures radical inequalities in the distribution of power.

The radical pragmatism that Bruffee borrowed from Richard Rorty shares with other relativisms the inability or refusal to concede a superordinate value. If all knowledge is composed of "community-generated, community-maintaining symbolic artifacts" ("Social Construction," 777), the language of each community becomes a solipsistic circle of self-referentiality. The only standard by which propositions can be evaluated (a dirty word for Rorty) is their ability to win acceptance *within* individual communities, their ability to "work," in the pragmatic sense, to the satisfaction of those wielding power. This is why it was important for Bruffee to describe communities as groups of "knowledgeable peers." If communities are stratified, part of "working"—of "community-maintaining"—is a proposition's ability to confirm the existing social hierarchy in its power. What is alluded to here, of course, is the "power/knowledge" interrelationship of a discourse (in Foucault's terms).

To equate knowledge with conformity to an institutional discourse is ideological as well as epistemological, and the rhetoric of consensus is most handy to those whose oxen are *not* being gored. Epistemic discourse theory, at least one like Bruffee's that ignores the relative power differentials of the subjects constituting a discourse community, privileges the "gorer" over the "goree," or the status quo over dissent. Or to put it in terms of a social-epistemic rhetoric, the relativity of knowledge within discourse communities precludes the political activity of choosing the better over the worse in competing versions of knowledge. We have here a theory to justify the study of writing completely in terms of how it works, of how knowledge is constructed rather than of whether one construction is preferable to another. The achievement of community consensus subordinates individual to institutional authority.

SOCIAL-EPISTEMIC RHETORIC IN PRACTICE

In order to illustrate the way Bruffee's version of social constructionism has helped advance the interests of authority at the expense of political and ethical criticism, I want to examine in some detail two essays.[1] While both tell stories about how powerful institutions work, the rhetorical purposes of the stories are diametrically opposed to each other. In the first, Richard Freed and Glenn Broadhead are intent on showing how the material and discursive objectives of two institutions can be facilitated with the least possible resistance. In the second, William Donnelley seeks to offer the most effective ethical resistance possible to an institution's material and discursive objectives.

Freed and Broadhead apply social constructionism to the analysis of the discursive regimes of two international corporations. Their study examines the discursive practices of a management consulting firm that the authors (to preserve confidentiality) call Omega and an accounting firm they style Alpha. Alpha's "auditing culture" is codified in a "sacred text," or company manual regulating proposals. The main concern of the *Proposal Guide* is to avoid, in Freed and Broadhead's words, "promising a client that he will save a certain amount of money or realize a certain profit as a result of the *auditing* services" (158–59). By contrast, the consulting firm, Omega, must make specific promises about the results its clients can expect to receive as an outcome of consultation studies. Otherwise, both Alpha and Omega share a style and form of discourse common to the corporate "culture" in which they do business: brevity, initial informality, and "boilerplated," jargon-ridden contractual limitations (160).

Freed and Broadhead present Alpha and Omega corporations as discourse communities, operating in what they describe as "a context that conditions, governs, and constrains, not just the message, but the writer producing it" (162). It is at this point that the semantic vacuity of the term "community" becomes troublesome. The constraints on discourse at Alpha and Omega serve institutional needs. Each company relies on its sacred text because those at the top of the corporate hierarchy believe that codified discourse conventions are instrumental to the company's financial success. The rhetoric of community and consensus makes sense to the degree a community of interest among employees in fact exists. But it would be absurd to define Alpha corporation, in social constructionist terms, as a community of what Bruffee calls "knowledgeable peers" ("Social Construction," 777). There is nothing at Alpha or anywhere else in a capitalist economy remotely so democratic.

To the extent institutions wield power, they tend to be rigidly hierarchic and even authoritarian in their control of discourse, as Freed and Broadhead's study demonstrates for the two international corporations. One does not readily imagine a junior accountant walking into the Alpha boardroom to advocate that the firm start promising clients specific financial benefits in its accounting proposals. Clearly, at Alpha corporation, authoritative knowledge, far from being arrived at by parliamentary debate among knowledgeable peers, is established by the board of directors and imposed on employees at successively subordinate levels in the organizational hierarchy. To call any arrangement like this a discourse community is simply to confirm the dominion of bureaucratic authority. And I believe it is safe to generalize from Freed and Broadhead's study that most institutions are undemocratic and that, for most members (employees), a high degree of conformity is necessary to survival. The authority of knowledge, therefore, is used to maintain the dominance of the corporate power structure. And to the extent we teach our students a rhetoric that speaks of this process as a consensus reached in a community of knowledgeable peers, we are submitting to bureaucratic domination.

Thus, social constructionism as it is most often understood in composition studies enables students to identify with institutional objectives, to assimilate themselves to authoritative discourses and organizational hierarchies. But can social constructionism authorize "abnormal discourse," discourse that contests the dominant articulation of institutional objectives?

To examine this process of dissensus in rhetorical action, I want to turn to an essay that attempts to dispute the reigning consensus of its author's discourse community, William J. Donnelly's "Medical Language as Symptom: Doctor Talk in Teaching Hospitals." According to Donnelly, the clinical vernacular used in teaching hospitals, and in the medical profession generally, dehumanizes patients. They are treated as faceless medical "cases" and blamed for their "complaints" (in this country's culturally approved practice of blaming victims for their suffering). In medical discourse, for example, a patient with falling blood pressure is said to have "lowered his blood pressure."

As part of this dehumanizing process, patients are reduced to the passive subjects of biomedical authority (87). In Donnelly's words, nearly everything said about the patient in a typical clinicopathologic exercise in the *New England Journal of Medicine* could be said as well for a lesser primate with remarkably good health insurance. The message is clear: disease counts; the human experience of illness does not. (88)

The reason for this inhumanity, Donnelly believes, is that medicine's "ruling paradigm views a world of objects, not experiencing, interacting human beings" (88). Facing an entrenched consensus of knowledgeable peers, he advocates a new emphasis on medical ethics in the curricula of medical schools. There would be new required courses in which students would read books like Kuhn's *Structure of Scientific Revolutions* as an antidote, Donnelly writes, "to the notion that science offers immutable knowledge." Medical students would also study "literature, drama, and film as well as autobiographical accounts of both illness and doctoring" (91).

What is to be noted here is that Donnelly's dissent from the consensus of his discourse community must draw not only on knowledge (on constructions of reality) from outside his discourse community but also on knowledge of a different *kind* from his community's vernacular: literature, drama, film, and autobiography. These alternative cultural texts ("social artifacts," as Michael Walzer calls them) will inevitably embody standards of justice opposed to those dominant in the authorized discourse of biomedical practice. It is not that Donnelly wants students to acquire more medical knowledge: he seeks, rather, "a new vocabulary, one that does not simply add knowledge but also enlarges consciousness" (91). What he wants is precisely what neopragmatists like Bruffee dismiss as "foundational" knowledge, a rhetorical position from which the consensus for treating patients like lower primates can be challenged. What he wants is not "social construction" but ethical *deconstruction* of the authoritative knowledge enthroned in biomedical discourse communities. His community's very own sacred texts are at the heart of Dr. Donnelly's rhetorical problem. For in them, instrumental knowledge is privileged over ethical knowledge, as it no doubt is in Alpha's proposal manual and, indeed, in most institutional regulations in our society.

Bruffee's pragmatic emphasis on writing for business and professional "communities" has helped sanction discipline-specific composition courses as well as cross-curricular writing programs. This would be all to the good except that "practical" writing too often becomes formalistic attention to conventions and constraints explicit in "the way things are done" at places like Alpha and Omega. And at the same time, the ability to critique sacred texts (in Freed and Broadhead's sense) and dominant practices is too often slighted.

This conservative or "instrumentalist" appropriation of social-epistemic discourse theory has been resisted by a number of "writing across the curriculum" (WAC) proponents, including Patricia Bizzell, who more than a decade ago (as we have seen) called for a composition pedagogy based on sociolinguistic analysis of conventions at work within academic discourse communities. She believed that such an approach "would foster responsible inspection of the politically loaded hidden curriculum" ("Cognition," 238). Six years later, however, in a CCCC panel discussion entitled "Writing Against the Curriculum," Bizzell argued that WAC programs were being used not to examine the politics of institutional discourse, as she had hoped, but to sanction the hidden curriculum as part of the aim of instruction.

Some already have begun to advocate replacing traditional first-year rhetoric and composition with technical, business, or professional writing courses. One extreme proponent of teaching academic and professional discourse conventions as formal reflections of discipline-specific realities has argued that English departments have no legitimate claim to supervise freshman composition, let alone WAC programs. Catherine Pastore Blair amplifies disciplinary discourse conventions into particularistic "languages" and "cultures" (an abstraction of material forces similar to Bruffee's). And Blair is not merely being metaphorical. She writes: "Just as German is no better a language than French, English department writing is no better than writing in anthropology. It is only better by its own local standards" (384). She holds that "each of the disciplines is a separate culture" and that "separate linguistic communities will never understand each other fully" (385–86).

On the basis of this argument, Blair rejects any claim that English departments should be considered "the experts in all writing" (385). However, the English department's claim to expertise rests not on its relationship to "language" or "writing" in the abstract (nor certainly to specialized knowledge of any kind), but on the fact that it "houses" the study of rhetoric, and therefore of analyzing and constructing persuasive arguments in written texts. Rhetoric also has traditionally been concerned with the politics of discourse, and one consequence of separating it from writing instruction is practically to guarantee that knowledge would serve institutional rather than public interests. Discipline-specific discourse encourages, in Bizzell's words, "the treatment of one community's discourse conventions as if they simply mirrored reality" ("Cognition," 238). The international corporations of Freed and Broadhead's study are examples of this relationship between institutional interests and conventions of discourse.

Of course, rhetoric and composition studies is responsible for knowing and teaching the ways of the world. The world works to a large extent by collaboration and cooperation, by filling out forms that guarantee efficient transfer of information. But our students need to know as well for whom the world is working, which is to say that we should want them to understand the implicit power relationships inscribed in written discourse and to be able to resist, revalue, and reinscribe the order of things.

To do this, however, we must avoid particularizing each discourse in its own disciplinary wrapper and accept that defining culture and language in terms of institutional interests is an argument against changing the apportionment of power. Arguments for change are heavily dependent on *ethos*, on moral suasion, as Chaim Perelman has pointed out. Unlike routine practices of discourse (Rorty's "normal discourse"), dissent cannot readily be formalized. It draws on standards of justice embedded in each culture (understood here in a global, not a particularistic, sense). Definitions of justice are, in Walzer's words, "social artifacts . . . embodied in many different forms: legal and religious texts, moral tales, epic poems, codes of behavior, ritual practices" (48). These textual sources of dissent must, by their very nature, transcend local boundaries of institutional discourse.

There is a civil need in a democracy to maintain a public sphere in which the continuous argument over justice can occur. It is precisely this function that is most seriously threatened by the fragmentation of "culture" into bureaucratic institutions like international accounting firms and teaching hospitals. Rather than limiting our students to an understanding of discourse as the formal practice of assent to "conventions," we should be elaborating a theory of dissent for composition pedagogy. This theory would begin, I believe, with a reinvigorated study of ethos.

As a theory of discourse, social constructionism offers students the means to conform to the mandates of institutional power, as Freed and Broadhead's study of international corporations illustrates. But it provides no rhetorical strategy for opposing institutional authority. As Donnelly's argument testifies, dissent customarily requires ethical arguments that are, to use Bruffee's pejorative term, "foundational." As already implied, I believe that all ethical argument is necessarily foundational, being accessible to the present only in an ongoing argument over the interpretation of a culture's texts. Ethical traditions exist in the cultural and historical con/text, beyond the jurisdiction of institutional authority. Good rhetoric and composition pedagogy requires a theoretical justification for dissent like Donnelly's. The rhetoric of social constructionism, at least as presently constituted, stacks the deck in favor of institutional domination and reinforces the solidarity of consensus against any advocacy of change.

The course of social-epistemic discourse theory since the mid-1980s illustrates our society's disposition to embrace pragmatism as a means of avoiding conflict. Traditionally, Americans have valued the pragmatic both in the general, utilitarian sense of optimizing tangible results (economic rationalism) and in the more philosophical sense of making optimum tangible results the measure of policy. This approach, however, begs the question of who will define the optimum, a decidedly political question. To teach writing as a discipline-specific information technology optimizes the interests of top management and major stockholders of corporations like Alpha and Omega. It may even maximize the salaries of students who learn to conform as enthusiastically as possible to sanctioned discourse conventions as "mirrored reality." But on the other hand, it is quite possible that training rhetorical "Good Germans" may stifle the accidents of "abnormal science" that we call innovation. More important, it seems to me, is the danger that a strictly conventionalist rhetoric, incompatible with traditional ideals of a liberal education, is very likely dangerous to a democratic polity and is certainly injurious to the interests of those excluded from the boardrooms of institutional power. Nevertheless, while social constructionism cannot itself offer any purchase for critique of dominant knowledge regimes, it can authorize the writing instructor to examine critically the politics of disciplinary discourses.

ETHICS AND THE REDISTRIBUTION OF KNOWLEDGE

The common curricular pattern in introductory writing instruction is to teach students to write the personal, self-expressive narrative and the expository essay arranged around the traditional rhetorical patterns (comparison and contrast, division and classification, cause and effect, etc.). Except for efforts to introduce multicultural and other "political" themes into reading and writing assignments, the first half—usually a semester in duration—of composition instruction has attracted relatively little theoretical attention. Of more interest to theorists has been the second half of the composition sequence, often referred to as the "research paper course." This space in the curriculum has increasingly been reformulated and marketed as an introduction to academic writing or, more specifically, to writing across the curriculum (WAC).

Often this is merely a semantic change, traditionalists in the English department continuing to teach a menu of disembodied "skills" like filling out note cards and introducing quotations properly, in some cases still in the bastard genre of cut-and-paste "research" on literary texts. But where the second-semester writing course has begun to be informed by rhetoric of inquiry or rhetoric of science, new openings to revolutionary post- or counterdisciplinary practices are starting to suggest themselves. At these junctures, it is possible to imagine reformulating composition as a rhetorical practice serving to democratize knowledge by subjecting it to the informed, ethical will of the citizenry.

Because the introductory composition sequence is most often the initiatory opening in the curriculum, writing instructors preside over the reinvention of the university (in Bartholomae's oft-cited phrase) for each student. We, perhaps more than any others in the university, set the terms according to which students orient themselves to the multiple discourses of disciplinary knowledge, the "subjects" our students study. Nearly all of us engaged in this project (the initiation into academic literacy) want to preserve as large a realm as possible for each student as a valued person. That is a large part of our ethos as professionals. Most of us also aim to equip students with the intellectual competence to take an active civic part in a more humane and democratic polity (however our vision of that polity might differ). Both of these desiderata, it seems to me, propel us toward a program that I am describing here as the redistribution of knowledge: a rhetorical understanding of inquiry (a social-epistemic concept of knowledge formation) that authorizes the subjection of knowledge to political and ethical responsibility. In a word, to justice.

The politics of knowledge making, therefore, should be a central concern of courses that aim to introduce students to academic discourse(s). The "rhetorical turn," which is part of the more general critique of positivism—going on across, between, and against disciplines—has begun to obviate the traditional distinction between scholarly inquiry and political commitment (ideology). Conceptions of what counts as a proven fact, a logical proposition, or a reasonable inference are seen to be socially constructed, "culturally, vocationally, and historically variable," in Herbert Simons's words (13).

While I plan to focus in the rest of this chapter and in the next on the rhetoric of inquiry in the social sciences, it should be noted that such sophism has infected the "hard" sciences and even mathematics. Knowing is knowing how to persuade, knowing the arguments. As two mathematicians write, part of being a qualified expert in, say, algebraic number theory is knowing which are the crucial points in an argument where skepticism should be focused; which are the "delicate" points, as against the routine points, in an argument; which are the plausible-seeming arguments that are known to be fallacious. . . .

The passage from the assertion to the acceptance must proceed ultimately by extra-logical criteria. (Davis and Hersh, 62, 67)

In many disciplinary discourses, knowledge and ethics continue to be dichotomized as separate realms of the objective (science) and the subjective (belief). Such a distinction persists even in our own field. The editor of a prestigious journal in composition studies remarked, in critiquing an earlier version of this chapter, "I sensed many places that felt like assertion rather than interpretation—places . . . that could have the impact of making people think of your article as an 'opinion piece.' " Here, "assertion" and "opinion" mark the devalued subjective pole of the binary, the realm of ethics and politics. "Interpretation" marks the objective pole, the realm where readers would respect my words as knowledge, not "mere" opinion. But as Michael Shapiro puts it, "what appear to be primarily denotative or descriptive accounts harbor mythologies, stories whose details and overall structures are designed to motivate conduct that accords with the authority and power that the mythologies defend and legitimate" (368). In rhetoric and composition studies, a reigning—but increasingly contested—mythology is that knowledge is politically and ethically neutral, that it can be written as "interpretation" without the taint of subjective "opinion." Of course, the editor was only offering his judgment about what would prove rhetorically effective in our "knowledge community," not arguing an epistemological position. Still, that estimation from one so knowledgeable about our professional peers indicates the tenaciousness of epistemic positivism.

Perhaps the most powerful model for a social-epistemic reform of composition studies (a reform integrating a politics of knowledge into introductory courses in academic discourse) comes from feminist criticism. My own teaching of the introductory "research paper course" has been fundamentally transformed by this work. The import of feminism for disciplinary and postdisciplinary knowledge can be well exemplified by the work of Donna Haraway, which might serve as a primer for the critique and redistribution of knowledge. Her method in, for example, *Primate Visions: Gender, Race, and Nature in the World of Modern Science* is one that the rhetoric and composition instructor can adapt to the design of any course in social-epistemic critical literacy. In brief, Haraway examines the knowledge-making process to expose the ways its accretion and validation vindicate the interests of groups dominant at a particular historical moment.

While the argument of *Primate Visions* is far too richly complex to outline here, one example might prove sufficient to illustrate how Haraway's critical feminism exposes the social-epistemic work of knowledge production in its cultural and historical context. Her account of primatology as a specialized bio- and paleoanthropological discourse growing out of post-Darwinian "natural philosophy" demonstrates the way history shapes knowledge. Part of the story, the part that will exemplify here the political exigencies of knowledge formation, treats the emergence of the "nuclear family" in post-World War II America. In Haraway's terms, researchers create and are reciprocally created by institutionalized "story fields" that are written to explain—and in so doing construct—primates (including preeminently *Homo sapiens*) as "natural-technical objects" (12) of knowledge:

Evolutionary discourse generally, and paleoanthropology and primatology in particular, are highly narrative; story-telling is central to their scientific project. . . . The stories taken together constitute a story field, with axes of organization and rules for producing transformations, distortions, and highlightings. These axes and rules derive both from deep structural cultural patterns and from people's continuing daily struggles over meanings. (188)

Thus, rules for the disciplinary discourse are the outcome of history ("deep structural cultural patterns") as it takes shape in "people's continuing daily struggles."

One natural-technical object was "Man the Hunter," the creature of Sherwood Washburn's "new physical anthropology" first articulated at the Cold Spring Harbor Symposium on Quantitative Biology in 1950 and elaborated thereafter by Washburn and the many anthropologists he trained, an entire "apparatus of publishing, student careers, conferences, collaborations and funding" (Haraway, 203). Man the Hunter was the creation and guarantor of two human metanarratives: the biological universality of "mankind" and the origin of the family in the process of adaptation to carnivorous territoriality. Haraway makes it clear that making the hunt an organizing principle of human origins underwrites universal (i.e., white European) patriarchy:

in Washburn's integrating functionalist sense, . . . all of history, including all of settled agriculture, paled into insignificance in the face of the truly human way of life, pregnant with ultimate threat and ultimate promise. All men, all those who reproduce themselves with their tools, were equal in this primal and universal matrix of masculinist reproduction of the species. Hunting was not about getting enough vitamin B12. (217)

Man the Hunter (the natural-technical construct) explained the Cold War in the "natural" terms of aggressive territoriality; it naturalized patriarchy, the dominance of men, and the domesticity of women at a time when, as we know, women were leaving the wartime economy and producing the baby boom. At the same time, Man the Hunter was establishing new territory in burgeoning suburbs, from whence he might sally forth to the city and return with prey for the family. Thus, Man the Hunter underwrites much of the social mythology that continues to shape the lives of our students.

As an originary story field, Man the Hunter authorized the foundation of what were believed to be essential differences between the sexes: inherent differences mirror the sexual division of labor replicated in the hunter-gatherer dichotomy. The hunting of large mammals required males to evolve the ability for planning extended forays on the savanna. Men had to become *political*. Females merely had to pick up things locally; their skills remained, like those of primates of other species, *social*. Man the Hunter, therefore, naturalized the gendered division between the public and the private domains. Stories became, in Haraway's words, "social-material forces" (288).

Much of the most interesting work in primatology since the mid-1970s has been done by Jeanne Altmann, Adrienne Zihlman, and Sarah Blaffer Hrdy. Using insights from feminist theory and their practical experience, these women have helped destabilize the masculinist story field designated Man the Hunter and with it the mythic naturalness of the nuclear family as well (Haraway, 283). They have looked anew at primate social interaction, seeing clearly for the first time the behavior of female primates as actors in their own right, not "as resources for male action" (322). Here, as Haraway makes clear, exposing the politics of sexuality does not necessarily lead to better explanations (i.e., closer to some Adamic truth about life forms). It leads, rather, to more self-conscious explanations, explanations aware of the multiple social and material forces that shape the very questions to which we seek answers. Awareness of the politics of knowledge makes it harder to use knowledge to oppress people in value hierarchies according to some supposed "natural" attribute. The stories informed by feminist critiques of natural and social sciences tend toward emancipation rather than subordination. I believe that examining the social epistemology of stories historically, in terms of the political interests they advance, would help Dr. Donnelly persuade his profession to make medical technology more humane.

Instead of limiting students to the particularistic rhetorical practices currently authorized, instructors of introductory academic writing courses should follow Donnelly's prescription and provide their students with alternative standards, competing stories, of ethical judgment. This will involve "deconstructing" as well as appropriating the conventions of institutional discourses, that is, redistributing knowledge now only in the possession of those empowered to speak. A genuinely epistemic rhetoric should provide the resources to write both kinds of stories. It should be forensic, recognizing that all claims to know are temporary and interested; it should be skeptical, recognizing that each proposition is composed of a dominant claim and suppressed counterclaims. An epistemic approach to composition instruction will need to be sensitive to this balance, teaching the conventions of discursive practices while encouraging the repressed play of ethical opposition that facilitates their refutation.

NOTE

1. Portions of this chapter appeared in a different context as "Determinism and Dissent: Keeping Discourse Theory Open to Rhetoric," *CCTE Studies* 53 (1988): 29–33.

Chapter 8

Learning to Explain the "Inexplicable": Chronicle of an Introductory Academic Writing Course

In this chapter, I want to present a case study of an instructor—me—struggling with the problems of what is called "pedagogical application" of theory. The theory, in this case, is exactly the kind of critical, social-epistemic rhetoric that I attempted to articulate in the preceding chapter, a rhetoric informed by a materialist/feminist sensitivity to the (ab)uses of knowledge. The scene of this study is a second-semester introductory composition course that I taught in the fall semester of 1992. The primary written sources on which this quasi ethnography is based are (1) a journal I kept during the semester, (2) my syllabus and other handouts, and (3) student writing in a number of genres, including course evaluations.

Here is the official description (since revised) of the course, as it appeared in the English department's *Policy Handbook for Effective Writing I and II*:

Effective Writing II (3 credits) continues the expository writing experience offered in Effective Writing I and explores techniques of gathering, evaluating, and selecting source materials to be used in writing research papers. This course shows students how to analyze and synthesize sources effectively and to select a point of view for writing about them; it also explains how extended discourse is carried on. Methods used include careful reading and analysis of the organization and styles in selected non-fiction texts and application of this information to writing, further practice in the writing process, explanation of documentation, and experience in using the university library.

My journal begins as I contemplate this course description, trying to imagine how I can integrate the methodology I've been reading about—rhetoric of inquiry informed by feminist criticism—into a traditional "research paper" course like the one I'm supposed to be teaching.

August 18: I have the same feeling looking at this course description as I did reading the *Gorgias*. The purpose of this course is to teach what Socrates calls the "kind of speech which deals with the subject matter of [any] particular art"—while I want to make it, primarily, into a course in the kind of rhetoric Gorgias's foolish puffery represents as the "producer of persuasion" (Plato, *Gorgias*, 63–64). I want the students to see themselves and others—even, especially, "the experts"—as producers of persuasion. I want them to see knowledge not only as a means to exert power over nature or as a way to control people, but also as a way of "naturalizing" the control over people. This means I'm going to have to lean hard on parts of the course description: "evaluating . . . source materials, . . . analyz[ing] and synthesiz[ing] sources effectively and select[ing] a point of view. . . ." I want to enable expertise, which seems to be the course's overriding objective, but at the same time to make the students squeamish about its purposes and its consequences.

Professionally, this can be authorized as social-constructionism, teaching the conventions operating in (meaning "producing persuasion" in, to use Gorgias's phrase) the context of various academic "discourse communities." But of course, I want to accomplish much more than that. By the end of the semester, my students should understand not merely *that* knowledge is constructed, not only something about *how* knowledge is constructed in a particular discipline; they should have an inkling about the process by which social and material interests shape what counts as knowledge. Without understanding how those global interests operate in local knowledge economies, students will mistake instrumental knowledge for objective nature, beyond the pale of ethical (political) critique. Ideally, my course will teach them how to peel back the natural veneer of social and even natural science, so that they come to demand for themselves—as citizens of a democracy—the right to decide what policy expert knowledge authorizes (what it's "only natural" to do).

This seems particularly important if our students will inhabit Jean-François Lyotard's postmodern world, where the decay of "grand Narratives" (the traditional sources of ethical arguments) no longer protects us from "the arrogance of the decision makers—and their blindness" (63). The complexity of expert knowledge increasingly enables small elites to make political decisions over the heads of "lay people." A critical rhetoric of inquiry, on the other hand, aims to make students politically astute insiders in the knowledge-making process.

A critical social-epistemic rhetoric does not entail Gorgias's cavalier know-nothingism or his reductionist equation of truth with hype. On the contrary, a politics of inquiry maintains that knowledge is so valuable that it must be socialized, that the power to decide on the use of information must be redistributed to all citizens. The alternative is to allow elite research communities to turn into Manhattan Projects dropping moral and environmental Big Boys on us.

August 21: I'm going to focus the course on "rhetoric of violence." After reading Foucault [*The Foucault Reader*], the question of how "the truth" is brought into existence by discursive formations seems acutely interesting, particularly the process by which disciplinary knowledge communities "fabricate" the mass and serial murderer as a pathological object of knowledge. Or to put it more simply: How do the human sciences explain what causes people to perform "unspeakable" acts of violence? That question will drive students' research for the semester.

August 27: [The syllabus for Effective Writing II, including an outline of course assignments reproduced below, is completed. The primary textbook is Charles Bazerman's *The Informed Writer*, 4th ed.; more about this shortly.]

Course Outline

Sept. 8/10:   Bazerman, chapters 2 & 3: Annotation and Paraphrase
              Handout, St. George & Wallace, "A Rage Toward Women Con-
                 sumed Texas Killer"
              Reaction paper due Sept. 10

Sept. 15/17: Bazerman, chapter 4: Summarizing
              On reserve: Susan Brownmiller, *Against Our Will*, chapter 8,
                 "Power: Institution and Authority"
              Summary with paraphrase and quotation due Sept. 17

Sept. 22/24: Bazerman, chapter 5: Responding to Sources
              Scholarly journals; explanation of assignment
              Causal analysis paper due Oct. 6

Sept. 29/   Bazerman, chapter 6: Voices in Texts
Oct. 1:   Library orientation: Locating scholarly journals

Oct. 6/8:   Causal analysis of scholarly article due Oct. 6
             Presentations of causal analyses to class

Oct. 13/15: Bazerman, chapter 7: Purpose and Technique
Collaborative workshop: revising and editing "critical syntheses"
in class
Final draft due Oct. 16

Oct. 20/22: Bazerman, chapter 9: Synthesizing Sources
Proposal for research project due Oct. 22

Oct. 27/29: Individual conferences

Nov. 3/5: Bazerman, chapter 10: Writing the Researched Essay
Presentations of research topics

Nov. 10/12: Bazerman, chapter 12: Creating Knowledge
Rhetorical analysis: deconstructing tropes

Nov. 17/19: Bazerman, chapter 16: Writing About Theory
Rhetorical analysis continued
Paper due Nov. 20

Nov. 24/26: THANKSGIVING BREAK

Dec. 1/3: Final class presentations of research
Essay due Dec. 4

Dec. 8/10: Individual Conferences

Final draft of researched essay (with research log and all previous assignments) is due in my office Dec. 14.

August 31: The syllabus looks pretty standard. Everything will depend on two things, only one of which I can plan ahead of time. The individual assignments must be written carefully and thoroughly before the semester begins (and, of course, revised during the semester as my heroic plans fall apart).

What can't be planned is my teaching persona(e). My "natural" interface with students is too directive and comradely to realize my pedagogical objectives in this course. Almost everybody, even my colleagues in the physical sciences, agrees that knowledge is "socially constructed," meaning that it's kind of a team effort. What they balk at is agreeing that it could be constructed a lot differently than it is. And the idea that those who aren't team members ought to have a voice in validating knowledge, they equate with the decline of civilization as we know it. I'll have to avoid making the tacit agreement with students that we understand the world in basically the same way and that I'm just extracting a certain amount of work from them in return for a grade. I'm going to have to play Gorgias, to work to demystify Socrates's credo of art without guile. Socrates's credo represents the dominant epistemology of our culture, shared by my students and most of my colleagues.

September 8: I started off the first class "epistemologically"—with a short writing assignment:

Explain what it would take to convince you that a person could use his or her will to float above ground (to defy gravity, to levitate).

We discussed this for about twenty minutes. Predictably, most of the students answered that they would have to "see it with my own eyes" and "look for the wires." I had to fight the urge to ask if that's all it would take, and eventually one student confessed that he wouldn't believe it even if he did see it with his own eyes: "I'd just assume somebody had tricked me and I couldn't figure out how." Then we talked about how we came to have such "faith" in the law of gravitation that—at the least—we'd have trouble believing our own eyes.

At the end of class I handed out copies of the syllabus and the first assignment: a copy of "A Rage Toward Women Consumed Texas Killer," a feature story by *Philadelphia Inquirer* staff writers Donna St. George and Linda Wallace, with the instructions

Read this report and try to focus on one aspect of your reaction to it. Then write a paragraph explaining this reaction to the class.

[I should summarize (and explicate) the news story here. It was written less than forty-eight hours after George Hennard murdered twenty-three and killed himself in a Texas cafeteria in October 1991. After a brief introduction establishing Hennard's hatred of women, the authors attempt to explain this animating rage, what they call his "bewildering anger." Hennard's suicide left "police to puzzle together the clues about what provoked his ruthless rampage." A second section, immediately following the introduction, supplies some of the details of Hennard's obsessive misogyny, most prominently his vision of "his mother's head on a rattle-snake's body." The third section, on Hennard's past, begins with a descrip-tion of the family's comfortable home in Belton, Texas, which "became George's house eight years ago when his parents parted ways, his father moving to Houston and his mother to Nevada."

The account then focuses on what was known in the immediate aftermath of the shooting about Hennard's parents and his childhood experience. A neighbor told reporters that Jeanna Hennard was an "attractive, well-traveled woman" but "found it peculiar that she never talked about her children." Another source said that Jeanna Hennard had admitted to him that her children were "alienated from her." Then James

Dunlap, a former roommate of Hennard's and source of the rattlesnake story, described her as "a high-strung, domineering woman who once came to blows with her son." Immediately following this characterization is "Hennard developed a 'very, very low opinion of women,' Dunlap said."

It is hard to avoid the inference that George Hennard's hatred of women was *caused* by his mother's high-strung, domineering personality. This interpretation seems implied because the text of the news story reports nothing of Hennard's relationship with his father beyond the following information: "[Hennard] was born in a Pennsylvania hospital where his Swiss-born father was serving his medical residency. . . . Georges Hennard served as a U.S. Army doctor for 22 years, moving his family as duty called. . . ." The text suggests that the father's significance to young George ended at birth, but it nevertheless recognizes Dr. Hennard's patriarchal proprietorship: it is *his* family that he moves as *his* duty—or "service," as it is rendered in the text—requires.

Taken together, these details focus attention on the mother's culpability, her responsibility for her son's "very, very low opinion of women." The father is exculpated by his very absence from the explanatory apparatus of the narrative, the nature of the "clues" with which we are left to puzzle together George's motives. Dr. Hennard's only presence in George's life is noted by a former landlord who told reporters, "They [George's parents] were fighting all the time, she and her husband were screaming, and the children were crying." Otherwise, the personal and affective—as opposed to the biological and legal—Dr. Hennard is absent from the text.

Beneath this sketchy narrative lies another account of what has gone wrong with George Hennard. The details selected to characterize Jeanna Hennard suggest the starkest of contrasts to the bloodless and imperturbable domestic model of motherhood constructed by post–World War II American mythology. Jeanna is seriously wanting in idealized maternal qualities: instead of being domestic, nurturing, private, and passive, she is well-traveled, high-strung, domineering, and gone—to Las Vegas, no less. And these qualities become the operative force, the putative cause, of her son's insane rage. The real villain of the news story becomes, at least implicitly, the mother whose abnegation of her "normal" maternal role— her place in the domestic and Oedipal economy—stands as the implied cause of Hennard's pathology.]

September 10: The class was divided into six groups of three to four to read each other's "reaction papers," which were due at the beginning of class. I asked each student to write down (1) what he or she believed was the cause of Hennard's killing spree and (2) what each of the other members of the group seemed to believe was the cause. Each group was then to formulate its own joint causal explanation. Finally, as a class, we attempted to formulate a statement about causation to which each member could agree.

As might be expected, all the students made the connection between Hennard's killing spree, his hatred of women, and his poor relationship with his mother. That much is assured by the text's selection and juxtaposition of the "facts." But once we got past the most general causal statements ("He did it because he hated women and people in general" and "George's anger was caused by bad relationships with women, especially his mother"), most of the class was stumped. Questions like "Why do you think Jeanna Hennard's personality would cause George to hate women?" or "What's the connection between having a very low opinion of women and mass murder?" got little response. Most students, when pressed for specifics, would say things like "It's impossible to know what's going on inside people's heads." Most believed that individual acts transcending what they considered "normal" were ultimately inexplicable. This seemed important for them to maintain, perhaps because a thorough search for the cause of such behavior must lead to a political indictment of social normality.

I was satisfied, however, that during the class discussion the idea of a "causal chain"—a pattern of asking "So what caused *that*?"—was established. And at the conclusion of class, I asked students to write a paragraph-long answer to the question "How would we find out what caused Hennard's mass murder spree?" This, I hoped, would focus attention on causal explanation as a rhetorical mode.

September 15: For the first twenty minutes of class, students exchanged papers and wrote a summary and a paraphrase with embedded quotation of a classmate's reaction paragraph (in preparation for the week's writing assignment). Then I asked several students (those who had written the most cogent reaction papers) to read their "methodology" papers. Several were quite fanciful: going to Hell to psychoanalyze Hennard or raising him from the dead to reenact particularly painful moments of his childhood experience. We then mapped out several methodologies that most of the class thought would explain extreme social pathology like Hennard's. They turned out to recapitulate the two competing metaphysical positions on mental events: the psychoanalytic and the physiological. Cause could be established by discovering either developmental trauma in childhood

("Deprivation of love in early years can create extreme emotional difficulties.") or physical abnormality ("Insanity is caused when something goes wrong in the brain.")

In general, environmental causation was by far the favored mode of explanation; the predominant method of investigating Hennard's homicidal anger was to amass details about his development by interviewing parents, siblings, childhood friends, former girlfriends, teachers, and even a resurrected Hennard himself.

Up to this point, it will be noted, the larger issue of cultural context was largely absent from attempts to explain causation. Motive forces were at the same time universal and individual; they were unmediated by culture. Thus, no one seemed to think it more than accidental circumstance that Hennard happened to have a pair of 9mm semiautomatic pistols with numerous multiple-round clips at hand. Fortunately, one student (Adam) had written the following in his reaction paper:

George Hennard was supposedly angry at his mother. He finally exploded, and took it out on all the people in the restaurant. Why was George so angry at his mother? It is impossible to understand this story unless we understand the normal family life with the mother staying home to raise the children. If the person had not watched television shows like *Leave It to Beaver* they wouldn't know why he was so upset.

After Adam read this passage to the class, we discussed the cultural ideal of motherhood and its supposed centrality to healthy childhood development. Because of the recently concluded Republican convention with its emphasis on "family values" (and the clash of role models offered by Marilyn Quayle and Hilary Clinton), the class was quick to pick up on Adam's insight about the cultural role of motherhood in providing a causal explanation for what went wrong with George Hennard.

September 17: Most of the class meeting was devoted to workshopping: students worked in small groups on editing and revising their summaries of the Brownmiller chapter. In the last ten minutes, I handed out the assignment to write an "evaluative essay" (which is due next week):

Write a paper (2–3 pages) evaluating Brownmiller's thesis by testing its power to explain Hennard's "obsessive rage." This means, of course, that you'll have to begin with a fair summary of its gist. Then, decide if her basic point can be extended to the circumstances of Hennard's assault on Luby's cafeteria, explaining why Brownmiller does or does not help us understand Hennard's motives.

[Brownmiller's "Power: Institution and Authority" (chapter 8, *Against Our Will*) is a rather shockingly explicit description of rape as a thoroughly institutionalized—and thus at least partially legitimate—exertion of patriarchal power to keep women in "their place" (i.e., inferior and subordinate). Drawing examples from homosexual rape in prison and the sexual abuse of children in the family, Brownmiller argues that rape, as she puts it in her introduction, "is nothing more or less than a conscious process of intimidation by which *all men* keep *all women* in a state of fear" (5). Of course, I want students to connect Hennard's individual "rage toward women" with the larger—if less visible and dramatically violent— operation of patriarchal oppression. And I will ultimately want them to confront the way patriarchy structures what counts as knowledge about the causes of violence in American society.

When I teach this course again, I will include selected readings from Simone de Beauvior's *The Second Sex* and from Angus McLaren's *A Prescription for Murder*, a study of a Victorian serial murderer, Dr. Thomas Neill Cream, and the social forces his career manifests.]

September 22: This class did not work! It became obvious at the beginning of our "discussion" of the Brownmiller reading that I had an agenda. I probably should have presented a lecture "illustrating" the function of Hennard as rogue patriarch, as Brownmiller's "conscious process of intimidation" gone berserk. Anyway, that's what I ended up doing. It's hard to tell from what they say whether they're "resisting" or the point is too obvious.

September 24: I spent today describing the scholarly journal and explain- ing its function in disciplinary knowledge. Illustrations were drawn from Greg Myers's *Writing Biology*. Then came the assignment to write an analysis of causation in a scholarly article. This is a copy of my handout.

Ascribing Causation in the Social Sciences
We have been examining how journalists establish causes—or explain motives— in our discussion of the George Hennard news story. We have been discussing as well what we as individuals think explains why Hennard killed 23 people. We have even looked at a theory that might be used to explain Hennard's behavior (Susan Brownmiller's). Now, we'll move on to examine how researchers in various disciplinary fields of study (especially psychology, sociology, and criminal justice) explain causes.

First, you should find an article from a professional journal—NOT A MAGA- ZINE—about multiple homicide. You should consult one of the print or on-line bibliographies in the social sciences and look under a number of entries: the name of a killer, homicide, violence, aggression, murder, social pathology, etc. Ask a librarian at the reference desk for help if you don't know how to access and search a bibliographical reference guide.

Second, read the article; make two photocopies of it; then, read it a second time, marking each passage that refers to the cause of the homicidal behavior.

Third, analyze very carefully the way cause is established in the article: the terms used, the kinds of evidence offered, the methodology for establishing proof, etc.

Fourth, write a three–four page explanation of how your article represents cause. TRY TO BE CRITICAL: look carefully for assumptions about cause that don't seem logical or causal statements that don't really seem to explain the events they refer to. You'll need to start with a summary of the article and enough background information so we nonspecialists can understand your analysis.

Fifth, prepare a shorter version of your paper that you can read or deliver in class in two–three minutes (see Bazerman, pp. 92–93).

[The next class was taken up with a standard library orientation practicum.]

October 1: I handed out a copy of a scholarly article (Jenkins, "Serial Murder in England: 1940–1985") to small groups. Each group analyzed the article for causal attribution and evaluated the logic of the argument. In the final twenty minutes of the period, groups' findings were compared. There was much consensus, and I feel students are prepared to write their own analyses.

October 8: In their in-class presentations, students in general are not doing analyses as well as I had hoped. I realize now that this would have happened in our practice, in-class analyses of the Jenkins article had I not circulated from group to group, asking them to "look at the *wording*, not the outside *world* that the text refers to." I tried to explain to each that our understanding of the story's context—its meaningfulness—rests on common asssumptions (cultural patterns or conventions) that we share with the authors, and that the real objects of study are those nearly transparent assumptions, those patterns we recognize as meaningful, not the particular details that form the narrative fabric in which the pattern is woven.

But now, left to their own devices, students are slipping—as I guess is natural—from textual analysis to recapping the narratives in both their papers and their presentations. They want to retell the stories, the gorier the better, not take them apart and examine their construction. A good bit of class time has been spent reporting details of pet torture, one of the "traits" characterizing the profile of a mass murderer. I have tried to use this issue to underscore the distinction between direct causal claims ("unscientific" and, therefore, advanced only indirectly) and claims that experimentally controlled factors *correspond*. The question I asked over and over was "So what do you *infer* the cause was?" or "What do the authors seem to think caused this behavior?" or "Why did the authors choose to compare the characteristics they, in fact, did?"

October 15: During the class workshops this week, it's been possible to look at the journal articles students are analyzing and to talk to them specifically about their own papers. This allows me to ask specific questions about specific texts and to do a "perception check." Several students don't seem to have a clue: they haven't been able to move past summarizing or even paraphrasing their articles. I asked three students to meet with me tomorrow (Friday) and granted them extensions so they can work on their papers over the weekend.

I handed out the assignment for a "critical synthesis" paper, which reads as follows:

Drawing Together Multiple Sources in an Interpretation
This assignment asks you to use the scholarly article that you've analyzed as a beginning or focal point for examining the *interpretation* of an event or events: a specific mass or serial killer.

Find at least three articles on a multiple murderer. Then, compare how they suggest or impute or assume causal factors. In particular, look for factors that are *common* to all interpretations. Recall (and refer to) your work on the Hennard article.

The next step in the pre-writing process is to compare the causal interpretation of your case study (the three articles on "your" multiple murderer) with the causal interpretation of your scholarly article.

Finally, write a three–four page "critical synthesis" paper reporting your findings. This paper is important: you should think of it as the embryo of your seminar paper.

[The purpose of this assignment is to make students see the underlying cultural connections between "popular" knowledge and expert knowledge. There are two reasons I believe this is essential to the goals of this course. First, students need to hold in their own hands the invisible tissue, so to speak, of their own culture. When they can perceive a cultural pattern underlying textual representations, they will have taken up these filaments.

Second, this assignment attempts to demystify "expertise," or at least domesticate it, so that students will feel as free to criticize the authority of power/knowledge institutions as to reject "opinions" (a word that seems to refer precisely to knowledge claims without institutional force, things that can be disbelieved without consequence).

At the end of class on Thursday (October 15) I assigned students to write a proposal for their major research project, urging them to follow Bazerman's instructions and format (288–300).]

October 22: The two class periods spent on revision of the "critical synthesis" papers have gone well. As expected, problems continue to occur. There is a common tendency, mentioned before, to shift attention from textual analysis to narrative details. This slippage might well have been encouraged by my reference in the assignment handout to " 'your' multiple murderer." In any case, I found myself constantly exhorting students to "pay closer attention to the words on the page."

A few are still having trouble deciding whether an assertion is attributing causation; or, better, whether they can safely impute assumptions about cause to an author. In the middle of class today I posed this problem of inference for the whole class in the form of an assertion one student was puzzling over. She paraphrased her source in the following words:

This psychiatrist, Dr. James Brussel, studied the evidence of the Mad Bomber [George Metesky] and predicted everything about him. He was from East Europe and was in his forties. Brussel knew he loved his mother but hated his father from the way the Bomber rounded off the bottom of his Ws like women's breasts. Dr. Brussel even predicted that he wore double-breasted suits, which the Mad Bomber was wearing on the day he was captured.

What kinds of inferences about the author's understanding of causal relationships might be drawn from this text? We ruled out, in the first place, any kind of neurophysiological causal factors, reasoning that none of the characteristics could be *predicted* on the basis of an undiagnosed neurological disorder. The causal pattern suggested here, everyone agreed, was Freudian. Several students knew specifics about the Oedipus complex and related them to the text. One student pointed out the causal role assigned to Metesky's unconscious, which "caused" him to round off his pointed "Ws" and choose a particular clothing style.

By this point, two or three students were objecting to the credibility of the story, giving me the opportunity to shift the discussion to the issue of method: If a theory predicts behavior, doesn't the appearance of the predicted behavior confirm the theory? Not if another—and here is the key—more *persuasive* theory also explains it. Here I suggested that our

American culture of individualism militates against any notion that we're puppets of something called an "unconscious." We like the free-market economy of behaviorism better, and tend to dismiss the rounded "Ws" and the double-breasted suit as extraordinary coincidences. We tend to find more persuasive a conscious economy of punishment and reward, growth and development, the normal and the malign.

We also had a good discussion on Tuesday of Bazerman's chapter 9, "Comparing and Synthesizing Sources," which is important to the "critical synthesis" assignment. All in all, I see signs of real progress (and would probably miss them if I weren't writing all this down!). Students seem to feel increasingly comfortable moving back and forth between scholarly and popular discourse. More are joining the discussion voluntarily. They also seem to grasp the basic interpretive tendencies: the clinical (case study), the empirical (quantitative), the psychological (behavioral/developmental), and the psychoanalytic. I even hear the words "cultural pattern" every now and then. In both speech and writing, students are using more and more social science lingo (i.e., "discourse conventions").

October 30: A week of conferences is mercifully over. I discussed each student's proposal with him or her. It became clear in the course of the week that I will not achieve my objectives unless I can find a way to shift students into a critical mode. They (almost all) are using their "journalistic" sources on multiple homicide to *confirm* the conclusions of their scholarly sources. Only one or two question the findings that they've extracted from disciplinary journals.

For example, one of the better students, Chris, is basing her research on empirical studies of homicidal behavior, especially an article from *Journal of Clinical Psychology*: Kenneth G. Busch et al., "Adolescents Who Kill." This study concludes that "the homicidal juvenile can be differentiated [from the control group] with these four symptoms: most importantly, criminal family violence and gang participation, but also alcohol abuse and severe educational difficulties" (484). Chris has discovered from her research that the subject (Albert DeSalvo, allegedly the Boston Strangler) fits this profile in specific ways.

It occurred to me in the middle of our conference to ask her to trace the causal chain back a link or two: "What causes violent families?" Or in the studiously empirical language of the Busch article, "What characteristics differentiate criminally violent families from other families?" Since the Busch study controlled for factors of age, race, sex, and socioeconomic status, I asked Chris to tell me what other characteristics she thought would differentiate violent from nonviolent families. Her considered answer was "religion," in the sense of church membership rather than religious teachings that constrained violence. From church membership we moved to more general characteristics of community that have been "broken down" by social changes in recent decades. So the question that I left Chris with was this: "How satisfied are you with the explanation that 'criminally violent families' are a major causal factor in adolescent homicide?" What I asked her, in other words, was whether an analysis of social forces like the decay of religious institutions or cultural patterns like the American proclivity to settle disputes violently would provide a better, more persuasive, causal explanation of teenage homicide than the educational and criminal justice statistics and census data that yielded such categories as "criminal family violence" or "severe educational difficulties."

[From my conversations with Chris and the other students during the conferences, therefore, I came to see that my assignment for the major research project had to include a step to foster dialectical thinking. That meant getting students, in the course of the prewriting stage (*invention*), to compile a list of factors that *might* better explain motivation or causation but that the student's sources didn't report at all or mentioned only in passing. That assignment reads as follows:

Instructions for Writing the Major Essay:
Evaluating Disciplinary Knowledge
In this major writing assignment you are going, first, to explain how, then to evaluate how well, expert knowledge makes sense of apparently senseless violence: that is, how well a "discourse" explains causation. All of the writing you have done so far this semester, as well as our upcoming "Tropological Analysis," will provide sources that you can incorporate in this longer essay (12–15 pages).

THE STEPS

1. Identify your "knowledge community." This is done by establishing a "nomen-klatura"—a network of scholars whose work is cited over and over in the journals you use. You *must* use four or more scholarly articles. With this list and some help from the library's reference staff, faculty members in different departments, and me, you can name your knowledge community (criminal justice, clinical psychology, neurology, psychiatry, etc.).
2. Identify and define "key words," the names your sources use for their major explanatory concepts. Be sure (a) to give the "popular" equivalent—how the

concept would be expressed in everyday conversation—and (b) to analyze them as "tropes" (which you will be practicing in the weeks ahead).

3. Summarize the major causal factors that your sources (and, by inference, their knowledge community) use to explain multiple homicide. *Then*, and this is essential, list all the factors that *might* explain cause or motive, which your sources *don't* use. It is this process—basically, comparing the two sets of factors—that you will be formulating in your thesis.

4. In one or two sentences, write a statement of your thesis as clearly and completely as you can. Your thesis statement will be an "evaluation" of what counts as knowledge in the community you are studying. It is your personal and *informed* judgment, which you will be presenting as persuasively as possible in your essay.

5. Organize the presentation of your argument around the causal factors in (3), your thesis statement (4), plus your discussion of each factor. Plan to work in material from other papers at specific points.

6. Compose a rough draft of your essay. *Then* revise it carefully and hand it in on November 20.

I handed out these instructions at the beginning of the first class after conferences.]

November 5: To begin the week, I gave a brief overview of Bazerman's chapter 10, "Writing the Research Paper," and explained how my assignment (above) departed from the process described in the text. Students didn't ask many questions, which worries me. I'm afraid they're overwhelmed.

Things improved when student presentations began. Each student had been instructed to state a "research question" (the extended answer to which would be the major essay) and to explain the progress made in answering it. While the students' presentations often lacked the specificity I'd hoped for, the class performed well its critical job of pointing out fuzziness and ambiguity.

In the final ten minutes of class today, I handed out the "Doing Tropology" assignment and explained briefly what tropes are and how one goes about "deconstructing" them.

[At this point, it's necessary to explain briefly how I understand "tropology." Following poststructural literary critics like de Man and Derrida, I assume that all language is tropological, in other words, that there is no real, positive distinction to be made between the categories "literal" and "figurative." It is, rather, that "literal" marks the authorized and accustomed use of what was once figurative, the process of troping being none other than the linguistic accommodation to ultimately material—or, in another word, historical—change.]

Here is the handout I gave students before we began the two-week short course in tropology:

Deconstructing Tropes in Academic Discourse
A "trope" is a transfer of meaning from what is a "word's" ordinary and principal usage (which we call the "literal" meaning) to some new or less usual one. Explaining what is new in language that is old (or the unknown in terms of what is known) makes the use of tropes essential in meaning-making. Metaphor and simile are the most common tropes.

A close analysis of the tropes in your article can tell you what the author (and, by inference, the larger knowledge community) *really* thinks about the object of research, sometimes more accurately than the writer could do consciously.

Think of your article as a series of metaphoric clues from which you can piece together another text, another partially hidden meaning, not just about the topic itself but about the author's assumptions, beliefs, and values.

This assignment requires you to select one of the scholarly articles that you are studying for your major essay and to do a rhetorical analysis of its tropology. Here is a brief guide for doing your analysis and writing it up:

1. Identify as many tropes as you can.
2. Find a pattern or patterns in your source. Are hurdles leaped, milestones reached, finish lines crossed, etc.? A race, then, is a controlling figure.
3. After isolating a major tropological pattern, OVERTHROW IT! You do this by writing an extended paragraph about the article's topic, using a different pattern of tropes. Instead of a race, for example, try a harvest, a sea voyage, or a seduction.
4. Finally, write an essay (about four pages) explaining the one or more controlling figures in your article and giving examples of them. Explain what you think they reveal about the author's attitude toward his topic and toward the wider world. What does this attitude reveal about American culture at the end of the twentieth century?

November 19: This is a reflection on four classes devoted to teaching students to recognize and "deconstruct" (in very rudimentary ways) tropes. I began (on November 10) with an explication of the figuration in the St. George and Wallace news article about George Hennard. Like most newspaper journalism, the text relies heavily on well-used metaphors: Hennard stews and broods; he is full of venom and hurls obscenities; his rage is triggered and consumes him; and so on. Students had little trouble discerning these rather obvious tropes.

But incredulity settled in when we began to pick at the very substance of language, at words like "rage" and "obsession," on which the text relies, not as one ornament easily replaced by another but as the necessary signs—guarantors—of the reality we share with the authors and with each other. The more sophisticated students seemed the most outraged at my calling into question the representational "propriety" of language. They resorted immediately to what Patricia Parker calls "little progress narratives," according to which we consciously "coin" new terms and thus fix their meaning (69). As one student blurted out, "It's crazy to say that a word could mean almost anything!"

And looking back on the last two weeks, it did seem crazy. It has been extremely difficult for me to play the "doubting game" with language. One can never "just" answer a question, which would allow closure. Discussion takes on a kind of adolescent preoccupation with double— often sexually suggestive—meanings. This makes me uncomfortable, and it brings out the immaturity of some in the class. Sometimes it all smacks of a facile solipsism. Nevertheless, I will impose a false analytic order on the direction of class discussion during the last two weeks.

I began by handing out a list of "contested tropes" to the students, words and phrases that implied or stated causal factors. I noted, for example, that the word "rage," as in "rage toward women consumed Texas killer," pointed toward a causal proposition; that much was clear. But the class could not agree on what rage signified, except that it was "a kind of anger." Rage, we discovered, descended from *rabere* and thus shares a common root with "rabid." This seemed to offer a reasonable interpretation: the Texas killer was consumed by—used by, or taken up into—a kind of mental or moral disease.

Was it reasonable, however, to imagine a series of events, an autobiography, provoking a man into a homicidal rage toward women? And if we were following this line of reasoning, hadn't we already shifted the efficient cause, as Aristotle would say, in the cafeteria carnage from Hennard to "women"? In other words, didn't the story's headline mean, in terms of primary causation, that *women* "consumed Texas killer"? That in our culture a "rage toward women" signifies a commonly understood, an understandable, cause of violence? And finally, wasn't the text "readable" to us because we all tacitly believed that the cause of "rage toward women" *is* the "domineering" woman?

Well, of course, the answer was "no." I was "reading too much into" the text, which in any case was about a "diseased" individual: "each individual case is different." Now, a student pointed out, there are even female serial killers.

At the end of class on Thursday (November 17) I summarized our disagreement in the following way: "Most of you believe that 'rage toward women' is an internal or private disease of the individual killer's mind. I am arguing that 'rage toward women' must be, first, a cultural disease that we all can 'read'; otherwise, it would make no sense to us individually." We all did agree that the meaning of words was often, as it is here, contested, and that to understand a text fully, we must focus on how its words "put" its conflicts.

[During the penultimate week of class, students gave short presentations of their papers, which were turned in on December 4. Then, after reading and commenting on each essay, I met with students one final time in individual conferences. In looking over my journal for these weeks, I see reemerging the themes that have been considered both here and in chapter 4.

The two problems most debilitating to my course objective—making students aware of the constructed, and therefore political, nature of knowledge—concern the stubborn refusal to generalize from individual instance and the Scottish commonsensical faith in the objectivity of language. In the first case, as the final papers demonstrated, most students refused to recognize that cultural determinants shape the predisposition to individual violence. Practically speaking, they ignored the readings and discussion of Brownmiller's thesis: that patterns of violence in our culture are essentially the means by which men (even male feminists) are assured dominance over women. When the evidence reaches an unavoidable level of preponderance, as with the fact that nearly all serial killers are men and their victims women, students have recourse to nature: men are naturally more aggressive, violent, concupiscent. As this study has repeatedly argued, culture is not an available category of students' epistemology.

It follows from their insistence on interpreting social behavior from the individual point of view that language must be largely an unproblematic system linking the subjectivity of the person with the object world it inhabits. In this regard, however, students demonstrated much willingness to question the verities of the learned discourses they were critiquing. Occasionally, I worried that this willingness was a symptom of American anti-intellectualism, but most students were able to make reasonably cogent arguments for their "deconstructions" of tropes and their critiques of knowledge making.

Overall, then, most students were willing to critique the research of knowledge communities, whether quantitative or qualitative, but they were unwilling to make causal counter-claims on their own, always accepting patent generalizations like "Every case is different" or "Male violence is driven by their hormones."

While nearly all students wrote critical essays that demonstrated an understanding of how a particular knowledge community establishes causation—no small accomplishment, in my judgment—several wrote genuinely sophisticated critiques. I would like to describe two, one that examines a "research logic" and one that focuses on the ideology of such a paradigm.

Kevin investigated a number of articles drawn from the *American Journal of Psychiatry* and the *Journal of Clinical Psychology* that reported empirical studies of homicidal adolescents and children. He began by trying to disconfirm the hypothesis that family violence is an *effect* rather than a primary cause of homicidal acts by young people, which most of the research purported to be the case (Lewis et al.; Busch et al.). Kevin wrote:

The reader of the research articles already has to believe that a violent family environment causes the children to become murderers. The research itself makes it just as easy to believe that the murderer or some other outside factors caused the family violence as [that] the family violence caused the murderer. It is just that our culture makes it seem unquestionable that bad parents cause bad children.

Kevin went on to "deconstruct" the causal explanation endorsed by his sources by means of a quite plausible hypothetical narrative according to which the child-subject's neurological (i.e., physiological) abnormality caused the family violence that one of his sources (Lewis et al.) assigned as a precipitating cause. In focusing on the causal role of family violence, Kevin pointed out how researchers often covered their flanks by mixing neurological and environmental characteristics. He called attention to the use of language to blur or "fudge" causal attribution, as in the term "Biopsychosocial Characteristics," which supplied the title for one of his sources (Lewis et al.).

In his most interesting insight, Kevin pointed out that a prominent convention of empirical/clinical psychological research is the avoidance of direct statements of cause. Researchers use an entire vocabulary of causal implication in which causal factors become "neuropsychiatric antecedents," "associated . . . presence," "common characteristics," and so on. But while observing this prohibition against the metaphysics of the cause-effect relationship, research often smuggled it in by the back door, writing about prediction and even prevention of violent behavior.

While Kevin did not use "culture" as a critical point of departure, several students in the class did. The most effective (from my point of view) was that of Patience, who examined the scholarly treatment of serial murder in the criminal justice literature. In a particularly astute critique, Patience (married and the mother of three) analyzed the use of what she called "domestic horror stories" by researchers to establish the cause of homicidal behavior. She illustrated this pattern with an explication of an article in *Federal Probation*, "Serial Murderers: Four Case Histories," by Temple University criminologist Faith H. Leibman.

Leibman explores, in her words, "the psychological profiles of a select group of serial murderers [Bundy, De Salvo, Kemper, and Brudos] in order to determine the common emotional and environmental backgrounds of these individuals" (41). The common factors are then boiled down to a list of seven developmental characteristics. The three heading the list are (1) "cruel and extremely violent parenting," (2) "a rejection in childhood by the parents," and (3) "a rejection by a member of the opposite sex in adulthood." Since, as Leibman concedes, "victims are almost always female, and their killers are almost always male," the "opposite sex" is a euphemism for women (42).

The article concludes that "parental abuse and rejection were major themes in the lives of these serial murder[ers]" (42). Patience points out that the word "parents" is rapidly elided to "mother" in the text: all four killers "saw the expression of anger toward their mothers as being of life-threatening proportion since the blood bond of mother and child was the only bond that was permanent in their lives." "Essentially," Leibman argues, "anger at their mothers repressed from childhood . . . was displaced onto their victims." Bundy's mother "did not offer the emotional support he needed." De Salvo was grotesquely abused by his father, but "his mother was unable to supply enough love and attention to make up for this abuse." Kemper's mother "continuously belittled him and punished him with physical constraints." And Brudos "was the product of a hostile, angry, sometimes violent father and a mother who did not really want him" (42–43). "As a mother," Patience writes with considerable irony, "I already feel guilty that I have done all of these things to my sons."

Patience continues by pointing out that the interpretive schema of the text—the primary significance of the "blood bond of mother and child"— cannot fail to create the impression that traditional domestic arrangements, which include women's material and emotional servitude, are necessary to avoid the creation of homicidal monsters. Absent or abusive fathers are passed over—at least as causal factors—in silence, as the simple reality of social life. "It is almost like fathers are condoned for being absent or violent," Patience comments, "because it is a cultural pattern. It is a joke that women's shelters are filled up every year on Superbowl weekend."

Patience recognizes as well the culturally sanctioned indictment of mothers like Jeanna Hennard (and, as a returning student preparing for a new career, herself) in the conclusion of her essay: "How can a mother ever know if she is giving enough emotional support or love? This is unfair to mothers. Fathers are at least as much to blame for violence, but mothers receive all of the blame."

While Kevin and Patience achieved the course objectives better than other students in the class, everyone incorporated elements of criticism that I had hoped to achieve. Some used rhetorical analysis to critique the research logics of disciplinary knowledge, as Kevin had done. Others, like Patience, used cultural criticism to uncover the unconscious presuppositions of paradigms. What did the students think of the course?]

March 27, 1993: Today I received my student evaluations of Effective Writing II for the fall semester. As usual, I'm keenly disappointed. In going back over my course journal, I can see that there were rough spots, places where the students did not seem to know how to proceed. Well, now I can confirm them. Nearly half agreed with the statement "Instructor did not make course objectives clear." And the same proportion disagreed with the statement "Instructor made good use of class time." Nor would many want to take another course in this subject. On the other hand, I got high marks for "Instructor got the students to think for themselves" and "Instructor was always available to help." I console myself with the thought that teaching against the grain like this is probably never going to win any awards, no matter how adept, adroit, and charismatic; it too aggressively violates the expected dynamics of authority in the classroom. For to become a Robin Williams (in *Dead Poets' Society*) means to place the student even more firmly in thrall to the material and ideological power of knowledge.

Chapter 9

Theology and Composition: Inscribing the Absent Other

A social-materialist rhetoric, as sketched in the preceding chapter, focuses attention on the often unintentional work of the political unconscious. It is reasonable to infer that this unconscious shapes a culture's most profound persuasion of what nature is (like) in ways compatible with existing social arrangements, which in turn come to seem "natural." Western dualism, for example, insists on the discursive space of subject and object, self and the stuff of otherness. In this historical context, therefore, any reenvisioning of composition as a culturally subjective process must address the textual regulations for inscribing alterity at and beyond the limits of the material world, the meaning of the Other as a metaphysical complement of the Self. This chapter attempts to explore the theological ground rules—the code of presuppositions, or Burkean "god-terms"—that govern meaning making in the contemporary composition classroom.

The way I have been using the word "culture" up to this point assumes that discourses, in anthropologist Terence Turner's words, "must be understood and analyzed primarily as constituents of contextually and historically situated social interaction" (123). Repeatedly I have written here about institutional structures of discipline and authority (with a general but until now unacknowledged debt to Foucault) and of hegemonic social relations that mediate the material reproduction of wealth, privilege, and power. In this final chapter, however, I want to examine the cultural context of writing and writing pedagogy from what might well be considered an idealist, rather than a material, position. Such a point of view assumes that "individual tropes and symbols constitute the fundamental units or elementary forms of culture . . . in abstraction from concrete social activities" (Turner, 123). If the preceding chapters must acknowledge their Marxist ancestry, the argument that follows is related to Max Weber, in particular the Weber of *The Protestant Ethic and the Spirit of Capitalism.* It will insist that ideas (here, religious ideas) are not merely superstructural but that they acquire an independent and indeed causal role in history.

Theologies begin with Absence, the chaos of a universe before the Word. Clifford Geertz describes the human need to displace Absence with meaning in the following terms:

[The] dumb senselessness of intense or inexorable pain, and the enigmatic unaccountability of gross iniquity all raise the uncomfortable suspicion that perhaps the world, and hence man's life in the world, has no genuine order at all—no empirical regularity, no emotional form, no moral coherence. And the religious response to this suspicion is in each case the same: the formulation, by means of symbols, of such a genuine order of the world which will account for . . . human experience. (108)

Thus, "creatural viability" (99) goads cultures to displace absence by "scripture." This is the genesis of the composing process, primal arche-writing, making present the self and the world by the "originary" writing of the Logos. It is what biblical inerrantists might mean by the "original autographs" of the Bible (see Boone, 33–35). Derrida insists on deconstructing this "self-presence of an onto-theological or onto-teleological synthesis" by making *"differance"* an inherent and intractible obstacle to recovering the originary trace of presence (*Positions*, 44). From this primal act of meaning-making began the process of "dissemination," the endless chains of supplements and substitutions in text, forever estranged from the transcendental, signified like Kafka's K. from the castle.

Yet the *Spur* or trace is there, eliciting a powerful desire for the absent Other, a desire that sometimes fissures Derrida's own text. In *Writing and Difference*, for example, he calls the trace a "transcendence beyond negativity" that provokes "a distress and denuding, a supplication, a demanding prayer addressed to a freedom, this is, to a commandment: the only possible ethical imperative, the only incarnated nonviolence in that it is respect for the other" (96; see Gunn, 50–51). I will begin, then, with some textual traces of desire that calls from across the great divide of alterity.

In his study of medieval monastic literary culture, *The Love of Learning and the Desire for God*, Jean Leclercq describes the interface between

literature and the mystical experience as one of impotence, "the inade-
quacy of what we say to represent what gives us our life"; for the mystic,
becoming aware "of this lack and this impediment is to intensify one's
desire to possess God fully. . . . The extreme frontiers of literature, therefore, open into the whole realm of the ineffable" (265). This longing for
the Other is not confined to the cloister but is abroad in the secularized
world of modern science as well.

The Nobel physicist I. I. Rabi writes:

When I discovered physics, I realized it transcended religion. It was the higher
truth. It filled me with awe, put me in touch with a sense of original causes. . . .
Whenever one of my students came to me with a scientific project, I asked only
one question. "Will it bring you nearer to God?" They always understood what
I meant. (quoted in Rigden, 73)

What Rabi meant, according to his biographer John Rigden, was that
experimental technique offered "access to fundamental insights and
fundamental knowledge about the world" (79), and the language of
molecular beams drew him closer to the ultimately unattainable margin
of the trace. In Rabi's words, "When I chose physics, I was no longer
practicing the Jewish religion, but the basic attitudes and feeling have
remained with me. Somewhere way down, I'm an Orthodox Jew"
(quoted in Rigden, 79).

Composition theory largely ignores this process of the cultural reproduction of orthodoxy. Unconsciously reinscribing the cultural text of
American individualism, it tends toward introversion by assigning auto-
inscriptions of the self. This metaphysical self-presencing through writing
cannot help but have a profound effect on our students' understanding of
their relationship to the Otherness of the world. The assignments they
receive in composition classes, as I argued in the opening chapter, most
often encourage them to take a self-reflexive stance against the outside
world, to construct their own "voice" as an expression of self and to "mask"
that construction by exteriorizing institutional discourses as instrumen-
talities that demand conformity in exchange for commodities and status.
In the process, the public or social dimension of individual identity, the
communal possibilities of encountering the Other, is practically written
out of existence.

In a world where economic, demographic, and environmental stress will
be making increasing demands on our students, teaching them either an
insular, self-referential discourse of privilege or an uncritical, strictly
instrumental one seems indefensible, at least to me, on pragmatic—let

alone ethical—grounds. A fully effective initiation into rhetoric requires that students be able to recognize their own "god terms." Let me illustrate from my own pedagogical experience how students can be fully immersed in a controlling theology and then suggest how a teacher might work toward historical self-consciousness.

DE-CYPHERING SIGNS OF POWER IN STUDENT TEXTS

Several years ago, I was offered an opportunity to read a set of student essays written for an interdisciplinary course at Texas Christian University titled "Religion and Politics in Latin America: The Cross and the Sword." This junior-level course, cross-cataloged as Religion Studies and Political Science, was taught by two professors, one from each discipline. I neither attended any of the classes nor met any of the students. Copies of their papers, names effaced, were given to me with the consent of class members. The project grew out of a conversation with one of the instructors about how poststructural literary criticism might inform our teaching practices.

According to the syllabus, the course focused on the "interaction of Judeo-Christian ideas and institutions with the society and politics of certain Latin American countries" from the perspective of "the cultural bases of North American presuppositions about religion and politics." The basic text for the course was H. McKennie Goodpasture's documentary history, *Cross and Sword: An Eyewitness History of Christianity in Latin America*. During the semester students wrote three "critical response papers" on assigned readings, the first, which I examine here, a personal reaction to an essay by R. M. Brown. According to the assignment, Brown argues that "because God is just, there is a moral dimension to history so that those who act oppressively . . . will be brought down and destroyed in the long run." The instructions continue as follows:

Write an essay in which you critically evaluate this argument, and then critically evaluate your own evaluation. That is, first state and defend a position for or against Brown's interpretation of how God "takes sides" in the Bible and today. Second, reflect on what elements *in your personal history and experience* lead you to regard the arguments for your position as decisive ones.

The assignment was provocative. Many students identified themselves both with the discourse of the Bible and with their own government's anti-insurgency policies in Latin America (or pro-insurgency policy, in the case of Nicaragua). They were confronted with Brown's persuasive argument that these two allegiances are in conflict and that "first world christians" are on the wrong side of the struggle for liberation. The papers as a group were thoughtful enough and earnestly engaged the issues of justice and power. Nevertheless, most were disturbing, to the course's instructors as well as to me. Of the seventeen essays I examined, fourteen seemed completely unable to understand the different cultures and material interests separating them from the Latin American subjects of their discourse—unable to reflect, in the words of the assignment, on what elements in their experience conditioned their interpretation of Brown's argument. (The authors of two of the remaining three papers identified themselves as Latin Americans.) The majority evaluated Brown's essay entirely in terms of their own individualistic values, that is, they were unable to write about the victims of Latin American oppression except in terms of their privileged position as "first world christians."

Rhetorically, the student texts resorted to the construction of a bounded *self* (a persona or voice) sharply distinguished from the *other* as the object of their discourse. One wrote, for example:

To take a side and defend it is to put myself in a very difficult position because . . . I have never witnessed the life of a third world resident. . . . With [Brown's] interpretation, I end up on the side of the oppressor, which I had never thought of before. Do I deserve to be destroyed and brought down eventually because I happen to be a citizen of a country involved in the oppression of another country? I am considered a Pharaoh because of where I live.

Here, an accident of birth appears to be the decisive issue in the interpretive act. What does not come before the eyes of the *self* seems outside the boundaries of one's moral responsibility. The scene of oppression, where one might witness "the life of a third world resident," is simply not "where I live."

Another student found that she or he could accept Brown's thesis by domesticating "the oppressed" into another, larger and more familiar, category—"the righteous":

Admittedly I am not an oppressed christian since I live in a country where religion and politics are separate. . . . My view of God supporting the oppressed, however is [comparable] to his similar support for the righteous.

Implicitly, however, the "oppressed christian" is a foreigner to be naturalized, clearly distinguishable from the domestic "righteous."

This dichotomy is often stated more explicitly:

Brown suggests that a theme of liberation for the oppressed runs consistently through the Bible but I would argue that the theme is more one of love and salvation. . . . Sure, it does depend on how you look at it, on where you are socially, economically and politically. A person raised and living in a militant environment will turn to passages in the Bible that relate to and comfort him or her. . . . I grew up in the United States, "the land of the free," so different passages from God's word relate to and comfort me. It is not so much a question of who is right in interpreting the Bible—me or a Latin American—because our circumstances are not even comparable.

The oppositional distinctions pervade the text: I/the oppressed; me/a Latin American; "the land of the free"/a militant environment; the individuated biblical message of love and salvation/liberation for the oppressed.

Grammatically, this distancing of *self* from *other* calls for frequent subjective and conditional predication, which is much in evidence in these essays—for example, when a student wrote:

Just because I am "rich" does not mean that God is against me. If I were being oppressed in a third world country, I would probably also focus on the Exodus story for hope.

Some students agonized over the dichotomy of *self* and *other* in the very process of inscribing it:

My personal struggle with all of this is that I can see Brown's argument, and I can support it—at least half of me can. The other half of me . . . applies literally all that the Bible states . . . including "love your enemy." But when applied to the everyday lives of the Latin American, [this injunction] seems to be "just a nice theory."

Another wrote:

I think that if I were a Latin American . . . , I would join the struggle; I would not allow myself to live with such humiliation and fear. . . . I cannot do any of that because I live in the United States. I am in a sense, spoiled.

Other students, however, passed over the divorce of *self* and *other*, apparently unaware of making it. When a student writes that "Christians are definitely obligated to give to the poor," the reader feels entitled to some relief that it is not the other way around.

One approach to the ideological individualism of these texts would be to deconstruct the signifier "God" as the sign of universal justice, turning it against the ruling practice of valorizing the *self* in binary opposition to the objectified *other* of the student texts. In fact, the students themselves occasionally authorized just such a deconstruction. One, who began with the assertion "God is just," later wrote that "God is with the oppressed as well as the oppressor. He may seem to be more with the oppressed because they need him more," and then concluded: "Taking sides does not coincide with a divine being." In this text, justice gradually slipped into dereliction.

Of course, some students dismiss the idea that we can know whose side God is on, invoking good historical reasons for their skepticism. More commonly, however, God takes both sides. One wrote, for instance, "I think each person's God helps them have inner strength to handle difficult problems when they arise." Relativism thus helps resolve the moral contradiction at the heart of the assignment.

The discursive strategies that I have been describing here are closely related to those Edward Said calls "Orientalism": the dominant discourse essentializes, dichotomizes, and estranges the *other*. Such textualizations, in Said's words, "function to suppress an authentic 'human' reality." The "orient" thus "coalesces as a field of representations produced by the discourse" of European orientalists (3). The discourse of Western humanism, which includes that of the liberal arts curriculum, creates an individual—perhaps a kinder, gentler, individual with refined sensibilities, a more caring ethos, but an individual nonetheless who divides the world into sedimented categories of *self* and *other*, the West and the Orient, the "I" and the "peasant."

Any critical revision of the "Cross and Sword" essays would have to begin, as I have suggested, by deconstructing this hierarchy of *self* and *other* that students have learned to write as a strategy of privileged discourse. In fact, the assignment asked students to evaluate critically their own arguments in light of their mediating *"personal history and experience."* This instruction was (mis)interpreted as authorization to privilege the presence of *self* in the self/other binary. Deconstruction offers a powerful technique for precipitating the kind of dialogue envisioned by the assignment's authors: reversing the privileged pole of the opposition.

Students might be asked to begin a critical revision of their essays by reinscribing them in the words of the absent *other*, perhaps as Salvadoran peasants who, as one student wrote, "go out to work in the fields every day, fearing the authorities will come and cut their heads off." Students might well be asked to imagine a genuine—that is, socially situated—dialogue (a rhetoric of difference) in which a "peasant" might say:

I think each person's God helps them have inner strength to handle difficult problems when they arise.

Taking sides does not coincide with a divine being. I was raised and am living in a militant environment, so different passages from God's word relate to and comfort me.

Just because I am "poor" does not mean that God is for me. If I were not oppressed in a third world country, I would probably not focus on the Exodus story for hope.

Because God is in control of history (Psalms, 96:10), if He chooses to allow a certain group to win, it is because it is His will.

Deconstruction is a prescription for overcoming the inside/outside dichotomies that make these words sound, at the least, ironic. In a world where radical inequality in the distribution of power exists, the very construction of *self* is, in effect, a distancing and marginalizing rhetorical move. If the object of that discourse is domination itself, the student is merely being asked to retextualize existing hierarchical relationships in accordance with the dominant rhetoric of consensus.

To the extent that we are teaching students this rhetoric, we are confirming them in the very ideology of individualism that obscures their own privileged place in the world. As the assignments discussed in chapter 1 indicate, we too often encourage students to use "personal experience" as evidence, present communication in Aristotelian terms of the writer "playing" an audience with a "message," and suggest that ethos (authentic voice) is something to be blended into a discourse like so much corn sweetener. As examples of student writing in upper-division liberal arts courses, these papers are an indictment of our own failure as teachers of rhetoric and composition to help students escape the prison house of self-referentiality. A pedagogy serious about critical reading and writing must teach students to de-cypher—both in the sense of decoding signs of power and privilege in texts and in the sense of demarginalizing signs of the *other*.

The experience of reading the "Cross and Sword" essays convinced me that the pragmatic ideology of individualism was so invisible to most of the student writers that it must somehow be conditioned by unconscious theological preconceptions that order for us, as Geertz maintains religions do in all cultures, "the way things in sheer actuality are." This metaphysical order of the world creates its reality out of haphazard contingency by tuning "human actions to an envisaged cosmic order" and projecting those "images of cosmic order onto the plane of human experience" (Geertz, 89–90).

To examine these presuppositions about what the world is like and subject them to rhetorical analysis—to help students unveil how they are, and others might be, persuaded about the nature of things—I sought to explore the sedimented religious pre-texts that underlie and perhaps control the operations of cognitive processes and discourse conventions. I want now to describe a pedagogical experiment that attempted to peel away the strata of textual accretions and to explore the theological substructure (with apologies to Marx) that naturalizes capitalistic economic rationality as the palpable shape of reality.

GRAMMATOLOGICAL RE-VISIONING OF THEOLOGY

There is, of course, a fundamental distinction between "revision," which is a formal or textual operation, an ex-pressing (pressing out what is already "on file" in the writer's personal experience), and "reenvisioning," which is a dialogical operation, a game for two or more players. Nancy Sommers has explicated the former with great clarity in her study contrasting the revision strategies of inexperienced student writers to those of experienced adult writers. Unlike most student writers, experienced writers have learned to "re-view," to create meaning by seeking, in the course of the composing process, "to emphasize and exploit the lack of clarity, the differences of meaning, the dissonance, that writing as opposed to speech allows in the possibility of revision" (Sommers, 386). Inexperienced writers, by contrast, revise at the surface level of lexical change. They fail to perceive semantic dissonances in larger structures, the dialogue of meanings at play in their own writing: "the incongruities between intention and execution" (385), which serve as a kind of autodialogical heuristic for experienced writers.

While Sommers specifically wants students "to see again" or to see differently, she (like most composition theorists) understands invention as techniques, however complex, for individual writers to use in private. The problem of perceiving dissonances is a cognitive one: developing ideas, defining terms, examining assertions, and so on. It seems clear that we are faced with more than the cognitive problem of "translating . . . thought to the page, the language of speech to the more formal language of [written] prose" (382). More particularly, if we are concerned to put students in some control of the cultural forces that shape the "sheer actuality" of their worlds, we must teach them to read not just semantic dissonances but cultural ones: like competition/violence or athletics/literacy in "Teacher Wins Big" or our national security/their death squads of the "Cross and Sword" essays. It seems to me that composition instruction should aspire to genuine intellectual engagement with issues, not merely to formal features of modification, specification, discursive multiplication of examples, and the like.

Hopes for reenvisioning a topic, as distinguished from revising an essay in the abstract, rest on developing rhetorical strategies for reading and writing texts suspiciously, looking with jaundiced eye and with some intuition about human motives, with some sense of the tragic incompatibility between disinterest and self-interest. In short, we want students to come at their own writing from multiple perspectives, but more especially from perspectives that their habitual modes of thought render invisible.

Instead, when students are assigned to revise, most resort merely to adapting their preinterpreted, Platonic understanding of truth to the demand for new discourse (see Ulmer, "Deprogramming"). Most of my students, for example, understand life as a competitive struggle in which expensive commodities are awarded in proportion to achievement of something they call "success." Asked to write on their aspirations in life, most specify "financial success," or some equivalent formulation, as the basic measure of their happiness. Although other of life's satisfactions— health, work, romance, family, even adherence to some religious or ethical ideal—are often accounted important, an inscription of a common scheme of values might come out something like this: "I want to be an attorney, making enough money to give my family the good things in life and to help others less fortunate." Underneath the decencies in which they have learned to dress their desires—"enough money" and "good things" and "others less fortunate"—lies the ideology of consumer capitalism. In this utopia, an instinctual, romanticized acquisitiveness drives an ever more abundant economy of more or less equal competitors. The successful are rewarded with "good things" while the rest of us are in proportion "less fortunate."

For students, dissonances in this system are impossible to perceive because, as Berlin argues, material and discursive practices are saturated in ideology

[that] provides the language to define the subject (the self), other subjects, the material world, and the relation of all of these to each other. . . .

Ideology always carries with it strong social endorsement, so that what we take to exist, to have value, and to be possible seems necessary, normal and inevitable—in the nature of things. ("Rhetoric," 479)

An ideology is always historically specific. The discursive formations most powerfully conditioning our students' interpretations of social and personal experience are an amalgam of cultural texts that would certainly include the economic rationality of Franklin's *Autobiography*, Emersonian individualism, Herbert Spencer's social Darwinism, and the pragmatic tradition of William James, John Dewey, and George Herbert Mead, among others, occasionally mitigated (or, as I will suggest in a moment, aggravated) by selective readings in the Bible. These and many others have been blended into a synthesis with a very hard surface.

In order to introduce some ideological fissures into this surface of student writing, I decided to formulate a pedagogy informed by the critical theory that I was reading at the time. If Geertz is correct, I reasoned—if religion invests a culture's model of reality with its patina of obviousness, the palpability of "sheer actuality"—then my students' writing must be structured in part by a metaphysical schema, a more or less secularized theology. And I theorized that such textual inscriptions could be deconstructed, revealing at least the outlines of that unconscious theological order.

Asked to interpret a simple apologetical work (the religious equivalent of vulgar Marxism), students ought in theory to reproduce the metaphysical properties of that exemplar in the terms of their own ideology. In other words, the assignment would elicit a simulacrum of ideology by reinscribing the theologically significant "graphemes" of the original text, thus opening up a field of play in the signifying system. Then we could compare pre-text and simulacra, creating in the process the kind of cultural dissonance necessary to genuine dialogue.

The text I chose for this exercise was a narrative essay titled "My Possible Dream," published in Norman Vincent Peale's *Guideposts* magazine in 1983. Before proceeding, let me summarize briefly the salient points of this personal experience narrative.

The author, Ms. Fran Roberts, begins her story with the dissolution of her marriage, consequent loss of her "six-room . . . place in the country," her enforced move to an apartment on the edge of what she calls a "rough neighborhood," her ex-husband's subsequent evasion of child support for their two children, and finally the collapse of her health. At the nadir of her fortunes, Roberts hears a radio evangelist telling her:

With God all things are possible, . . . but you need to know what you want. . . . Start by setting goals—but not fuzzy goals. You can't just say, "I want a nice house" or "I want a different job." You must be specific. Picture in your mind what you want. And *believe* every day. (20–21)

Roberts does just that. She creates a picture of her dream house, right down to details like an "L"-shaped front porch and an apple tree in the backyard. Then, as she puts it, she "turned the project over to God." Soon she is able to go back to work at a better job, as "an associate editor with a business publications firm in New York City" (21). The pieces begin to fall into place. A year after her return to work, Roberts gets a new job, working for a small newspaper in exurban New Jersey, where she finds the dream house. Her father, almost miraculously, presents her with money for the down payment and closing costs. The final impediment, the FHA's reluctance to guarantee a mortgage for a divorced woman (the events related in the narrative occur about 1970), is overcome by the intervention of a U.S. congressman. "In the years before equal loans for women were guaranteed by law," Roberts concludes, she "was able to buy the dream house she envisioned and God provided" (23).

The process of interpreting this narrative generated three separate written assignments, each followed by class discussion. Taken together, this work proceeded as a dialogue between my students and me, as it had to, since we began with widely divergent, if not diametrically opposite, ideological positions. The class in which this inquiry was conducted was, because of its religious orientation, composed primarily of more than usually privileged, middle-class freshmen, by tradition at least nominally Christian and predominantly of evangelical Protestant persuasions. I was trying to understand, I told them with fair candor, why we as Americans—who value equality so highly—ignore or at least tolerate radical inequalities in wealth and power.

The project began with an assignment to read Roberts's essay and respond as follows:

Is Ms. Roberts, the author [of "My Possible Dream"], a Job-like character whose faith in God is ultimately rewarded after long tribulations, or is she a selfish materialist who conceives of God as the great mortgage banker in the sky, or . . . what?

Make your own judgment about what kind of transaction is being described here, and explain it as clearly as you can in an essay. . . .

The initial set of student responses to this assignment took three basic forms that might be labeled reproduction, resistance, and translation of "My Possible Dream." First, two of the twenty-four students merely affirmed Roberts's own interpretation of the power and willingness of God to grant petitions of the kind her narrative describes. Two more were offended by the text's theological implications. One wrote, "It is doubtful that His priorities are what Mrs. Roberts feels they are. . . . It is as if God is some sort of Santa Claus, used year round." The other demurred more circumspectly: "I find it difficult to compare her to Job, as his problems were much more severe than hers. He had to deal with complete poverty and several deaths in the family."

As expected, however, fully three-quarters of the class translated the metaphysical order of the narrative, reinscribing it as a kind of meritocratic parable. Typical of the majority was this student's response:

Ms. Roberts was not a materialistic or selfish woman, but just not satisfied with her accomplishments in life. She was able to set goals for herself and use belief as a form of motivation to reach them.

Or, as a second explained:

I think maybe she was confused about what God had actually done for her. Mrs. Roberts believed that God gave her that "dream" home, but in reality all he had given her was the will power and determination to get out of her previous situation. She set a specific goal for herself and set out to achieve that goal. Anyone can accomplish anything they set their mind to.

While reinterpreting the author's version of events, these students often implied that Roberts had deluded herself. As a third writer put it, "Her success was not by faith alone; it was the desire and drive to better her condition." The echo of Luther's formula for justification, by faith alone, suggests the outline of the (seemingly) unconscious metaphysical relationship between spiritual salvation and worldly success present in students' theological subtexts, what Weber called "the spirit of capitalism."

"My Possible Dream" seemed to present a coherent metaphysical system in a completely innocent form. It made little attempt to cover over slippages in signification: from salvation to success, for example. That this text incorporated the theological substructure of American consumer capitalism (incorporating the "protestant ethic" into the "spirit of capitalism") seemed to be confirmed by the fact that so many students agreed substantially on a reinterpretation that in actuality deconstructed the central claim (the apparent authorial intention) of the text.

In the ensuing class discussion of the first writing assignment, I introduced the basic concepts of Saussurean linguistics—the arbitrary, and thus problematical, relationship between signifier and signified— and of Derridean *differance*, allowing us to place "under erasure" the agent in the events that had led to Roberts's acquisition of her house, the agent indicated in the text by the signifier "God." In the course of this discussion, we agreed that divine agency is actually missing from the text's truth claim, an absence that most student interpretations had recognized, implicitly at least, in phrases about Roberts's "drive to better her condition." According to the text, the narrator responds to the radio preacher "*as though* God Almighty was telling me I did have a prayer [of acquiring a house]" (emphasis added; 21). After her initial prayer, she "felt peaceful and secure, *almost as though* I had received assurance" (emphasis added; 21). Thus, the text presents God's agency as analogy for something else: her successes occurred "as though" God had ordained them.

Again, when Roberts finds her dream house, she says to God, "Now all I need is money for a down payment." As soon as she gets home, she calls her father to tell him about the wonderful house she has found (and, incidentally, needs a down payment to buy). Providentially, we might be tempted to think, her father has come into some money (having sold some riverfront property) and promises help with the down payment and closing costs. At this point, however, God's presence again evaporates from the text: Roberts reports, "I cried for joy; I was on top of the world. It had taken time and persistence, but my dreams were finally coming true" (22). Divine providence, the presence of which the text's very existence claims to validate, has absented itself, leaving Roberts's "persistence" as its only trace.

To read a text productively means, according to Derrida, "to dismantle the metaphysical and rhetorical structures which are at work . . . not in order to reject or discard them, but to reinscribe them in another way (quoted in Spivak, lxxv). This, it seems to me, is exactly what most of my students did, however unconsciously. They sensed (sharing the same historically conditioned theological expectations, or culturally specific regulations for interpreting experience) that the present signifier, "God," warrant of the literally authorized interpretation, was papering over an absent signified, which Roberts's text reveals as "persistence" at a crucial juncture in her narrative. Precisely at this point, the text calls its own privileged, authorial interpretation into question.

A perception of this disjunction showed up in formulations like those already quoted. Here is another example:

There is no clue as to how close her relationship with God is. . . . I believe that with determination, one can do anything. I think Mrs. Roberts saw her condition, did not like it, and decided to do something about it.

That something, as another student put it, was "to work her way up. She got better positions and started meeting people with a little more power." As a result of student interpretations of the "My Possible Dream" text,

Fran Roberts had come to inhabit an economy of reified commodity desires and hierarchical power relationships very much like the one our students are preparing to enter. Thus, the story that presents itself as testimony to divine providence ends up being read as an affirmation of American success mythology, a kind of Horatio Alger story (to which it bears obvious structural similarities). This could happen, it seems to me, if the "stories," as fairly interchangeable signifiers, shared a common metaphysical subtext in the minds of the majority of my students.

The class and I agreed that Roberts used the signifier "God" to refer to the agency providing her house. But just what was being signified, what trace of reality was being called up out of the world and into the text? The consensus that emerged in class discussion was that since "God" rewarded "persistence," both signifiers inscribed the same trace of reality (the "seek and ye shall find" text being comfortably accommodated to the market-place). Nearly the entire class was willing to agree to the following interpretation of the text: "Mrs. Roberts used her belief [in God] to achieve the goals she had set for herself." The two signifiers—providence and persistence—were equivalent for all but two of the students.

In the second writing assignment, I asked the class to revise—that is, to reinterpret Roberts's narrative—by placing not "God" but "belief [in God]" under erasure and by considering the reinscription in its place of "greed." The assignment read:

Go back and comb the text of "My Possible Dream" carefully. Then prepare a brief with your evidence for identifying the trace of meaning as either "belief in God" or "greed."

Papers and discussion resulting from this second assignment centered on the ethical evaluation of Roberts's story. No one was willing to argue that God rewards greed; but the majority of the class found that Roberts's desire (not to say obsession) for the house did not constitute greed. Many agreed with the assertion that, as one student put it, "Ms. Roberts wanted the best for her children," although that claim is never made in the text. And as another wrote, "In the eleven years after she acquired her house, Mrs. Roberts did not ask for anything else. Therefore, she is not a greedy person." The relatively modest price of the house seemed to exculpate Roberts in the minds of many.

There was some dissent. Some students argued that Roberts was greedy because she was "hung up on the house." One made the point that the narrator's obsession wasn't just with a decent place to raise her children in peace and security: "She never once said that she looked at the 'Houses for Rent' section in the newspaper." The consensus of the class, however, was that organizing one's spiritual life around the acquisition of a "home" (as the real estate industry has taught us to say) does not constitute "greed."

But what about social and political consequences of organizing one's life around the private acquisition of commodities? I wondered how this theology of persistence rewarded would accommodate those for whom success would indeed be miraculous. The third assignment in my inquiry asked for another reinscription of the class's proposition "Roberts used her belief in God to achieve the goals she had set for herself." This time, I asked them to examine the text closely for evidence that the trace signified by "belief in God" could not better be inscribed as "social class privileges" and to write a defense of their judgment from textual evidence.

In making this final assignment, I argued that the text itself admits questions about class privilege. The most notable example occurs near the beginning, where Roberts inscribes a set of what George Dillon calls "perverted commas"—quotation marks—that signal "exact sites where the word merges, recoils and intersects with the words of others" and "boundaries or gates where the words of the other enter, stand, and exit from the discourse" (68). They mark the inlet of intertext, a conscious use of encoded interpretation—a most obvious trace of meaning—that the author expects her audience to decode in a certain way, that is, according to a shared cultural pre-text. What, then, did my students, most of whom belong to relatively privileged strata of society, make of the marker "rough neighborhood"? Roberts uses this phrase to mark the edge of the social precipice on which she tottered before (as the students put it) "working her way up." I wanted to know if they perceived the class markers in the text by which the author separates herself socially from the inhabitants of "rough neighborhoods."

In the event, they could not. The written responses to and class discussion of the third assignment indicated an inability or refusal to admit significant social disparities. My students' "socio-logic," as Moffatt calls it, was "too impoverished" by their individualism (166) to seriously consider what seemed obvious to me: the existence of social and, in the case of "rough neighborhood," probably racial marginality that excludes others from the meritocratic competition.

Students simply refused to concede my argument that "rough neighborhood" signified those disenfranchised by reason of class and race and effectively excluded from the higher education necessary to get the "better jobs" requisite to realizing dreams like Fran Roberts's, that it signified those Americans without advantages like parents with valuable riverfront property and knowledge about how the FHA works, those without access to women's rights advocates and U.S. congressional representatives. My class would not (could not?) admit the unequal distribution of cultural capital, privileges conferred on Roberts, on them, and on me. They marked the inhabitants of the "rough neighborhood" with the same quality of Otherness that the "Cross and Sword" papers designated "peasants."

In the place of what I saw as a hierarchy of power and privilege, my students posited a free-market economy of "equal opportunity." The only difference worthy of note was the presence or absence of persistence, what my father used to call gumption. This faith was manifest in credos like the following:

> Where you start from isn't that important. Through the persistence that Mrs. Roberts showed, all people can work their way up to decent housing. A person from a low income neighborhood can go through the same process of hard work and faith. It may take longer, but Mrs. Roberts herself started from [the edge of] a "rough neighborhood."

WHAT GOD SAYS: FUNDAMENTALIST AND EVANGELICAL METADISCOURSES

As Bruce Lincoln has argued, discourse itself is hierocratic, the credible and authoritative myth having the power "to mystify the inevitable inequities or any social order and to win the consent of those over whom power is exercised" (4). There are always, however, counterhegemonic discourses available "to demystify, delegitimate, and deconstruct" the dominant mythos. While a rhetoric of difference focuses attention on the material interests of social power, the often unintentional work of the political unconscious—the very invisibility of differences (as exemplified by my students' reading of "My Possible Dream")— must be written into a discourse in the form of rules for determining what nature is (like). Western dualism requires the writing of a discursive space for both subject and object, the unified self and the stuff of otherness. Any reenvisioning of composition as the practice of cultural critique must therefore address the textual composition of alterity at and beyond the limits of the material world, the meaning of the Other as a metaphysical complement of self. It is at this level that students learn to reproduce the credible and authoritative myth.

It seems plausible, then, that there are rules for writing this myth, and rules as well for subverting it, in our historical-cultural archive. (Perhaps this is merely a roundabout way of saying that writing is always already situated in social and intellectual history.) Because these rules operate to

construct the "sheer actuality" of experience, I have called them theological. But there are competing (though unequal) theologies. The dominant
one, that which enabled the student interpretations discussed earlier in this
chapter, might be called a "fundamentalist" metadiscourse, or a discourse
of Transgression. It is transgressive, I would argue, in the sense that it
incorporates a fundamentalist protestantism, defining itself as the only
authorized interpreter of a univocal, unequivocal law, supposedly self-evi-
dent in the Bible. Since justice lies in enforcing the division between
obedience to and transgression of "God's Law," people are divided into
the righteous and the damned. Similarly, the law of property divides
Americans into the "persistent" and the transgressive inhabitants of the
"rough neighborhood."

   In contrast to this theology of transgression is what might be called
an "evangelical" metadiscourse, or a discourse of Inclusion. This I
associate primarily—but not exclusively—with African-American religious traditions. The evangelical expresses the historic interests of
African-Americans, material and spiritual, which have seldom been well
served by white people with exclusionary divine laws.

   The law that divides humanity into the righteous and the transgressors
is "the Word of God." As Kathleen Boone has argued, fundamentalism (of
whatever stamp) is not so much a set of beliefs as a set of discursive rules
for interpreting a text, in this case the Bible. Although these rules are
presented as expounding the "plain sense" of the text, they are primarily
institutional, resting on communal authority vested in preachers and
commentators: "authoritative interpreters are able to exercise power over
their subjects by effacing the distinction between text and interpretation"
(78–79). One of the most deeply rooted rules of fundamentalist biblical
interpretation is that "human efforts to effect changes for the good are not
only utterly futile, but by definition contrary to the divine plan. . . . It is
the business of the Christian to evangelize individual souls, not to engage
in social or political activism" (53). The way things are is the way God
intended them to be.

   Thus, when the Bible "says" things like "Blessed are the peacemakers,
for they shall be called the children of God" (Matthew 5:9), the discourse
calls for a distinction between public and private morality: individually,
we should "turn the other cheek"; nationally, we should maintain a strong
nuclear deterrent. In her study of religious life in Amarillo, Texas, A. G.
Mojtabai has amply documented this discursive division into "us" and
"them," into collocations of selves and others. As one of her informants
explains during a conversation on war and the Beatitudes, taking a human
life is

foreign to everything I belive in. But, at the same token, don't you break in my
house, I'll kill you for it. In *concept*, in conviction, my moral standards, I am a
conscientious objector, but I'm going to protect myself, my life, my family. And
if it takes taking your life to protect it, I'm going to do it. . . . I don't feel there's
any conflict at all. Because one is concept, and one is practicality. (77–78)

Dr. Winfred Moore, pastor of Amarillo's First Baptist Church, makes the
same distinction more theologically:

if you read the *whole* of the Bible, you'll discover that, while God is a lover of
peace, the God of peace, He is also a man of war. . . . Sometimes God has to use
tough love because there are some people who will not listen, who will not heed,
who will not obey. And, you see, I happen to believe also that God *did* command
Saul to destroy the Amalekites. (131–32)

This marking off of the transgressor, the housebreaker, or Amalekite,
serves as political authorization for the status quo. In a sermon titled
"Christian Citizenship," Moore explicated Paul's injunction to civil
obedience (Romans, 13) in these words:

Everybody must obey the civil authorities that are over him, for no authority exists
except by God's permission. The existing authorities are established by Him, so
that anyone who resists the authorities sets himself against what God has established. (127)

While only a small fraction of our students hold specifically fundamentalist beliefs like these, my argument is that the "sheer actuality" of the
law (whether it be human nature, God's Word, or free-market economics)
and the dichotomy it establishes between the obedient and the transgressor
is historically embedded in the cosmology of various discourses we share
as privileged ("fundamental") subjects of American culture. Edward Said
locates the source of what I have been calling here a theological "metadiscourse" in the "imaginative and emotional need for unity, a need to
apprehend an otherwise dispersed number of circumstances and to put
them in some sort of telling [moral] order" (*Beginnings*, 41). But this need
for unity is experienced differently by marginal groups who are most often
the Others or objects of the dominant culture.

Rev. Vernon Perry, who presides over the largest black congregation in
Amarillo, complained to Mojtabai in political terms about the ascendance
of fundamentalism among his parishioners. According to Perry, "The black
community, that can least afford to be conservative, is more conservative
than the white folks here. . . . They've taken on the color of the larger

community" (Mojtabai, 107). Implicit in this remark is the recognition that African-Americans' interests require a different kind of discursive order. When one's immediate ancestors have been slaves, one takes little comfort in divine prohibitions of social change and mandates punishing transgressors of the law.

The discursive universe that I have styled the "evangelical" metadiscourse draws on a host of rhetorical strategies that can be best exemplified in the work of Dr. Martin Luther King, Jr. In contrast to the litany of moral decline that, for the fundamentalist, demands obedience to the status quo, King represented the world as essentially beneficent, guaranteeing the ultimate victory of good over evil. Instead of the "End Time" emphasis on Armaggedon, and Christ's returning to judge, "rightly dividing" the saints from the condemned, King's rhetoric played on the theme of Christian redemption. "I Have a Dream," for example, is King's personal statement of faith in the inevitable arrival—*in history*—of the day when social divisions between people will dissolve in a divine communion.

The law for King was "Unearned suffering is redemptive." Keith Miller explains this law as follows:

In a beneficent cosmos, unearned suffering *automatically* pays long-term dividends. The unearned suffering of the Hebrews under the Pharaoh *made inevitable* their eventual arrival in the Promised Land. Christ's unmerited crucifixion *inexorably* implied his resurrection. The suffering of American slaves *impelled* the signing of the Emancipation Proclamation. . . . The Christ event is ultimate because it both enacts and illuminates the underlying, recurrent meaning of all history. Essentially, King told blacks that their unearned suffering did not refute Christianity but instead re-enacted it and thus reaffirmed it. (259)

"Truth," according to Foucault, "is linked in a circular relation with systems of power which produce and sustain it, and to effects of power which it induces and which extend it" ("Truth and Power," 74). King's advocacy of civil disobedience extended the tradition of both black and white protestant pulpit oratory. As Miller has shown, King "borrowed" his rhetorical power from "homiletic commonplaces," but he also transformed this material into an effective weapon for social and political change (250). The metadiscursive law governing this powerful transformation is inclusion: the Others of the discourse are transformed from "persistent" transgressors into a genuine community of God's children. Private division into "nice" and "rough" neighborhoods is refigured as a public feast at which the children of slaves and those of slaveholders share communion together ("I Have a Dream," 219). The system of power that had been realized in the truth of the transgressor is thereby made to induce and extend King's own vision of racial equality. This, it seems to me, is *real* reenvisioning.

If the cultural text shaping the construction of the world for most Americans in the late twentieth century is still governed by a "white" metadiscourse of exclusion, it is no wonder students can perceive little dissonance in their convictions of the essential fairness of American society. I have argued that a genuine dialogue about difference, about the self and its writing of the Other in terms of class, race, and gender, is basic to conserving traditional values of liberal education in an increasingly commodified "information" society. Only by reversing the self/other polarity (reenvisioning, that is, from a cultural perspective) can the signification of "equal opportunity" be deconstructed and reinscribed as a rhetoric of material equality.

Historically, I have suggested, we might imagine the cultural context of writing instruction in theological terms, as an extended half-life in the decay of seventeenth-century religious doctrines: the soul decomposing into the self, and individual salvation into success. The remains of these cultural templates seem to underlie American individualism and undermine any serious consideration of social or collective alternative. Perhaps only by reenvisioning and rewriting our cultural text as the material and discursive outcome of history (a critical process for which the composition class seems ideally suited) can American higher education move beyond personal and economic self-indulgence and prepare students for the kinds of global challenges that must preoccupy the world in the twenty-first century.

Bibliography

Amariglio, Jack, Stephen Resnick, and Richard Wolff. "Division and Difference in the 'Discipline' of Economics." *Critical Inquiry* 17 (1990): 108–37.

Arlen, Michael. *Sixty Seconds.* New York: Farrar, Straus, and Giroux, 1980.

Bartholomae, David, and Anthony Petrosky. *Ways of Reading: An Anthology for Writers.* 2nd and 3rd eds. Boston: St. Martin's Press, 1990, 1993.

——— . *Resources for Teaching* [Ways of Reading: An Anthology for Writers.] 2nd and 3rd eds. Boston: St. Martin's Press, 1990, 1993.

Bauer, Dale M. "The Other 'F' Word: The Feminist in the Classroom." *College English* 52 (1990): 385–96.

Beale, Walter H. "Richard M. Weaver: Philosophical Rhetoric, Cultural Criticism, and the First Rhetorical Awakening." *College English* 52 (1990): 626–40.

Berlin, James A. "Comment." *College English* 51 (1989): 770–77.

——— . "Rhetoric and Ideology in the Writing Class." *College English* 50 (1988): 477–94.

——— . *Rhetoric and Reality: Writing Instruction in American Colleges, 1900–1985.* Carbondale: Southern Illinois University Press, 1987.

Bizzell, Patricia. "Beyond Anti-Foundationalism to Rhetorical Authority: Problems Defining 'Cultural Literacy.'" *College English* 52 (1990): 661–75.

——— . "Cognition, Convention, and Certainty: What We Need to Know About Writing." *PRE/TEXT* 3 (1982): 213–43.

——— . "Marxist Ideas in Composition Studies." *Contending with Words: Composition and Rhetoric in a Postmodern Age.* Ed. Patricia Harkin and John Schilb. New York: MLA, 1991, 52–68.

——— . "Thomas Kuhn, Scientism, and English Studies." *College English* 40 (1979): 764–71.

Blair, Catherine Pastore. "Only One of the Voices: Dialogic Writing Across the Curriculum." *College English* 50 (1988): 383–89.

Boone, Kathleen C. *The Bible Tells Them So: The Discourse of Protestant Fundamentalism.* Albany: State University of New York Press, 1989.

Brantlinger, Patrick. *Crusoe's Footprints: Cultural Studies in Britain and America.* New York: Routledge, 1990.

Brooke, Robert. "Control in Writing: Flower, Derrida, and Images of the Writer." *College English* 51 (1989): 405–17.

Bruffee, Kenneth A. "Collaborative Learning and the 'Conversation of Mankind.'" *College English* 46 (1984): 635–52.

———. "Social Construction, Language, and the Authority of Knowledge: A Bibliographical Essay." *College English* 48 (1986): 773–90.

Bullock, Richard, and John Trimbur, eds. *The Politics of Writing Instruction: Postsecondary.* Portsmouth, NH: Boynton/Cook, 1991.

Burke, Kenneth. *Philosophy of Literary Form.* New York: Vintage, 1957.

Burton, Dwight L. "Research in the Teaching of English: The Troubled Dream." *Research in the Teaching of English* 7 (1973): 160–89.

Busch, Kenneth G., Robert Zagar, John R. Hughes, Jack Arbit, and Robert E. Bussell. "Adolescents Who Kill." *Journal of Clinical Psychology* 46 (1990): 472–85.

Clifford, James. *The Predicament of Culture: Twentieth-Century Ethnography, Literature, and Art.* Cambridge, MA: Harvard University Press, 1988.

Coles, William E., Jr., and James Vopat. *What Makes Writing Good: A Multiperspective.* Lexington, MA: D.C. Heath, 1985.

Connors, Robert J. "Composition Studies and Science." *College English* 45 (1983): 1–20.

———. "Overwork/Underpay: Labor and Status of Composition Teachers Since 1880." *Rhetoric Review* 9 (1990): 108–25.

Cooper, Marilyn, and Michael Holzman. "Talking About Protocols." *College Composition and Communication* 34 (1983): 284–93.

Davis, Philip J., and Reuben Hersh. "Rhetoric and Mathematics." Nelson et al. 53–68.

Derrida, Jacques. *Positions.* Trans. Alan Bass. Chicago: University of Chicago Press, 1981.

———. *Writing and Difference.* Trans. Alan Bass. Chicago: University of Chicago Press, 1978.

Dillon, George. *Constructing Texts: Elements of a Theory of Composition and Style.* Bloomington: Indiana University Press, 1981.

Dobrin, David N. *Writing and Technique.* Urbana, IL: National Council of Teachers of English, 1989.

Donnelly, William J. "Medical Language as Symptom: Doctor Talk in Teaching Hospitals." *Perspectives in Biology and Medicine* 30 (1986): 81–94.

Douglas, Wallace. "Rhetoric for the Meritocracy." *English in America: A Radical View of the Profession.* Ed. Richard Ohmann. New York: Oxford University Press, 1976.

Eagleton, Terry. *Literary Theory: An Introduction.* Minneapolis: University of Minneosta Press, 1983.

Ede, Lisa and Andrea Lunsford. "Audience Addressed/Audience Invoked: The Role of Audience in Composition Theory and Pedagogy." *College Composition and Communication* 35 (1984): 155–71.

Emig, Janet. *The Composing Processes of Twelfth Graders.* Research Report no. 13. Urbana, IL: National Council of Teachers of English, 1971.

———. "The Tacit Tradition." *The Web of Meaning: Essays on Writing, Teaching, and Thinking.* Ed. Dixie Goswami and Maureen Butler. Upper Montclair, NJ: Boynton/Cook, 1983.

Ewen, Stuart. *All Consuming Images: The Politics of Style in Contemporary Culture.* New York: Basic Books, 1988.

Faigley, Lester. "Judging Writing, Judging Selves." *College Composition and Communication* 40 (1989): 395–412.

Flower, Linda. "Cognition, Context, and Theory Building." *College Composition and Communication* 40 (1989): 282–311.

———. "Comment." *College English* 51 (1989): 765–69.

Flower, Linda S., and John R. Hayes. "A Cognitive Process Theory of Writing." *College Composition and Communication* 32 (1981): 354–87.

———. "The Cognition of Discovery: Defining a Rhetorical Problem." *College Composition and Communication* 31 (1980): 21–32.

———. "Problem-Solving Strategies and the Writing Process." *College English* 39 (1977): 449–61.

Foucault, Michel. *The Archaeology of Knowledge and The Discourse on Language.* Trans. A. M. Sheridan Smith. New York: Pantheon, 1972.

———. *The Foucault Reader.* Ed. Paul Rabinow. New York: Pantheon, 1984.

———. "Truth and Power." *The Foucault Reader.* Ed. Paul Rabinow. New York, Pantheon, 1984, 51–75.

Fraser, Nancy. "Sex, Lies, and the Public Sphere: Some Reflections on the Confirmation of Clarence Thomas." *Critical Inquiry* 18 (1992): 595–612.

Freed, Richard C., and Glenn J Broadhead. "Discourse Communities, Sacred Texts, and Institutional Norms." *College Composition and Communication* 38 (1987): 154–65.

Fulkerson, Richard. "Technical Logic, Comp-Logic, and the Teaching of Writing." *College Composition and Communication* 39 (1988): 436–52.

Geertz, Clifford. *The Interpretation of Cultures.* New York: Basic Books, 1973.

Giroux, Henry. *Border Crossings: Cultural Workers and the Politics of Education.* New York: Routledge, 1992.

Goodpasture, H . McKennie. *Cross and Sword: An Eyewitness History of Christianity in Latin America.* Maryknoll, NY: Orbis, 1989.

Graff, Gerald. "Teach the Conflicts." *South Atlantic Quarterly* 89 (1990): 51–67.

Gramsci, Antonio. *Selections from the Prison Notebooks.* Ed. and trans. Quinton Hoare and Geoffrey Nowell Smith. New York: International, 1971.

Graves, Donald H. "An Examination of the Writing Processes of Seven Year Old Children." *Research in the Teaching of English* 9 (1975): 227–41.

Guidelines for Avoiding Gender-Biased Language in University Communications. West Chester, PA: West Chester University. n.d.

Gunn, Giles. *The Culture of Criticism and the Criticism of Culture.* New York: Oxford University Press, 1987.

Hairston, Maxine. "Required Writing Courses Should Not Focus on Politically Charged Social Issues." *Chronicle of Higher Education* 23 (Jan. 1991): sec. 2, 1ff.

———. "The Winds of Change: Thomas Kuhn and the Revolution in the Teaching of Writing." *College Composition and Communication* 33 (1982): 76–86.

Haraway, Donna. *Primate Visions: Gender, Race, and Nature in the World of Modern Science*. New York: Routledge, 1989.

Harkin, Patricia, and John Schilb, eds. *Contending with Words: Composition and Rhetoric in a Postmodern Age*. New York: MLA, 1991.

Hillocks, George, Jr. *Research on Written Composition*. Urbana, IL: National Council of Teachers of English, 1987.

Harbrace College Handbook. 9th ed. 1982.

Harris, Joseph. "The Idea of Community in the Study of Writing." *College Composition and Communication* 40 (1989): 11–22.

Hodges, John C., and Mary E. Whitten. *Harbrace College Handbook*. 10th ed. San Diego: Harcourt Brace Jovanovich, 1986.

Jarratt, Susan C. "Feminism and Composition: The Case for Conflict." *Contending with Words*. Ed. Patricia Harkin and John Schilb. New York: MLA, 1991.

Jameson, Fredric. "On 'Cultural Studies.'" *Social Text* 34 (1993): 16–52.

———. *The Political Unconscious: Narrative as a Socially Symbolic Act*. Ithaca, NY: Cornell University Press, 1981.

Johnson, Richard. "What Is Cultural Studies Anyway?" *Social Text* 16 (1986/87): 38–80.

Kent, Thomas. "Beyond System: The Rhetoric of Paralogy." *College English* 51 (1989): 492–507.

Kidder, Tracy. *The Soul of a New Machine*. Boston: Little, Brown, 1981.

King, Martin Luther, Jr. "I Have a Dream." *A Testament of Hope: The Essential Writings of Martin Luther King, Jr.* Ed. James Washington. New York: Harper, 1986. 217–220.

Kuhn, Annette. *The Power of the Image: Essays on Representation and Sexuality*. London: Routledge & Kegan Paul, 1985.

Lauer, Janice. "Heuristics and Composition." *College Composition and Communication* 21 (1970): 396–404.

Lazere, Donald, ed. *American Media and Mass Culture: Left Perspectives*. Berkeley: University of California Press, 1987.

Leibman, Faith H. "Serial Murderers: Four Case Histories." *Federal Probation* 53 (1989): 41–46.

Lewis, Dorothy Otnow, Ernest Moy, Lori D. Jackson, Robert Aaronson, Nicholas Restifo, Susan Serra, and Alexander Simos. "Biopsychosocial Characteristics of Children Who Later Murder: A Prospective Study." *American Journal of Psychiatry* 142 (1985): 1161–66.

Lincoln, Bruce. *Discourse and the Construction of Society: Comparative Studies of Myth, Ritual, and Classification*. New York: Oxford University Press, 1989.

Lyotard, Jean-François. *The Postmodern Condition: A Report on Knowledge*. Trans. Geoff Bennington and Brian Massumi. Minneapolis: University of Minnesota Press, 1984.

Marcus, George. "Contemporary Problems of Ethnography in the Modern World System." *Writing Culture*. Ed. James Clifford and George Marcus. Berkeley: University of California Press, 1986. 165–93.

McGuire, Michael. "Materialism: Reductionist Dogma or Critical Rhetoric." *Rhetoric and Philosophy*. Ed. Richard Cherwitz. Hillside, NJ: Erlbaum, 1990. 187–210.

McLaren, Angus. *A Prescription for Murder: The Victorian Serial Killings of Dr. Thomas Neill Cream.* Chicago: University of Chicago Press, 1993.

Miller, Keith D. "Martin Luther King, Jr., Borrows a Revolution: Argument, Audience, and Implications of a Secondhand Universe." *College English* 48 (1986): 249–65.

Miller, Susan. *Textual Carnivals: The Politics of Composition.* Carbondale: Southern Illinois University Press, 1991.

Mischel, Terry. "A Case Study of a Twelfth-Grade Writer." *Research in the Teaching of English* 8 (1974): 303–14.

Moffatt, Michael. *Coming of Age in New Jersey: College and American Culture.* New Brunswick, NJ: Rutgers University Press, 1989.

Mojtabai, A. G. *Blessed Assurance: At Home with the Bomb in Amarillo, Texas.* Alburquerque: University of New Mexico Press, 1986.

Murphy, Peter F. "Cultural Studies as Praxis: A Working Paper." *College Literature* 19, 2 (1992): 31–43.

Murray, Donald M. "The Explorers of Inner Space." *Learning by Teaching: Selected Articles on Writing and Teaching.* Upper Montclair, NJ: Boynton/Cook, 1982. 3–7.

———. "The Interior View: One Writer's Philosophy of Composition." *College Composition and Communication* 21 (1970): 21–26.

Myers, Greg. "Reality, Consensus, and Reform in the Rhetoric of Composition Teaching." *College English* 48 (1986): 154–74.

———. *Writing Biology: Texts in the Social Construction of Scientific Knowledge.* Madison: University of Wisconsin Press, 1990.

Nelson, John S., Allan Megill, and Donald McCloskey. *The Rhetoric of the Human Sciences: Language and Argument in Scholarship and Public Affairs.* Madison, WI: University of Wisconsin Press, 1987.

Newmeyer, Frederick J. *The Politics of Linguistics.* Chicago: University of Chicago Press, 1986.

North, Stephen M. *The Making of Knowledge in Composition: Portrait of an Emerging Field.* Upper Montclair, NJ: Boynton/Cook, 1987.

Oakeshott, Michael. *The Voice of Poetry in the Conversation of Mankind: An Essay.* London: Bowes & Bowes, 1959.

Odell, Lee. "Piaget, Problem-Solving, and Freshman Composition." *College Composition and Communication* 24 (1973): 36–42.

Ohmann, Richard. *English in America: A Radical View of the Profession.* New York: Oxford University Press, 1976.

Parker, Patricia. "Metaphor and Catachresis." *The Ends of Rhetoric: History, Theory, Practice.* Ed. John Bender and David E. Wellbery. Stanford, CA: Stanford University Press, 1990. 60–73.

Plato. *Gorgias.* Trans. H. N. Fowler. *The Rhetorical Tradition: Readings from Classical Times to the Present.* Ed. Patricia Bizzell and Bruce Herzberg. New York, St. Martin's Press, 1990. 61–112.

Potter, Karen. "Teacher Wins Big in No-Pass, No-Play Lawsuit." *Fort Worth Star-Telegram*, 18 October 1988, 1, 7.

Reither, James A., and Douglas Vipond. "Writing as Collaboration." *College English* 51 (1989): 855–67.

Reisman, David. *The Lonely Crowd.* New Haven: Yale University Press, 1950.

Rorty, Richard. *Consequences of Pragmatism: Essays, 1972–80.* Minneapolis: University of Minnesota Press, 1982.

———. "Pragmatism and Philosophy." *After Philosophy: End or Transformation?* Ed. Kenneth Baynes, James Bohman, and Thomas McCarthy. Cambridge, MA: MIT Press, 1987, 26–66.

Rowe, John Carlos. "The Writing Class." *Politics, Theory, and Contemporary Culture.* Ed. Mark Poster. New York: Columbia University Press, 1993.

Rosenthal, Peggy. *Words and Values: Some Leading Words and Where They Lead Us.* New York: Oxford University Press, 1984.

Ryan, Michael. *Marxism and Deconstruction: A Critical Articulation.* Baltimore: Johns Hopkins University Press, 1982.

Said, Edward. *Orientalism.* New York: Pantheon, 1978.

Satten, Joseph, Karl Menninger, Irwin Rosen, and Martin Mayman. "Murder Without Apparent Motive: A Study in Personality Disorganization." *American Journal of Psychiatry* 117 (1960): 48–53.

Schilb, John. "Culture Studies, Postmodernism, and Composition." *Contending with Words.* Ed. Patricia Harkin and John Schilb. New York: MLA, 1991. 173–88.

Scholes, Robert. *Textual Power: Literary Theory and the Teaching of English.* New Haven: Yale University Press, 1985.

Shapiro, Michael J. "The Rhetoric of Social Science: The Political Responsibilities of the Scholar." *The Rhetoric of the Human Sciences: Language and Argument in Scholarship and Public Affairs.* Ed. John S. Nelson, Allan Megill, and Donald N. McCloskey. Madison: University of Wisconsin Press, 1987, 363–80.

Simons, Herbert W. "The Rhetoric of Inquiry as an Intellectual Movement." *The Rhetorical Turn: Invention and Persuasion in the Conduct of Inquiry.* Ed. Herbert W. Simons. Chicago: University of Chicago Press, 1990. 1–31.

Sloane, Thomas O. "Reinventing *Inventio.*" *College English* 51 (1989): 461–73.

Smith, Barbara Herrnstein. "Belief and Resistance: A Symmetrical Account." *Critical Inquiry* 18 (1991): 125–39.

Sommers, Nancy. "Revision Strategies of Student Writers and Experienced Adult Writers." *College Composition and Communication* 31 (1980): 378–88.

Spivak, Gayatri Chakravorty. "Translators Preface." *Of Grammatology.* By Jacques Derrida. Trans. G. C. Spivak. Baltimore: Johns Hopkins University Press, 1976. ix–xc.

Trimbur, John. "Consensus and Difference in Collaborative Learning." *College English* 51 (1989): 602–16.

———. "Cultural Studies and Teaching Writing." *Focuses* 1 (1988): 5–18.

———. "Essayist Literacy and the Rhetoric of Deproduction." *Rhetoric Review* 9 (1990): 72–86.

Tuchman, Gaye. "Representation and the News Narrative: The Web of Facticity." *American Media and Mass Culture: Left Perspectives.* Ed. Donald Lazere. Berkeley: University of California Press, 1987. 331–44.

Turner, Terence. " 'We Are Parrots,' 'Twins Are Birds': Play of Tropes as Operational Structure." *Beyond Metaphor: The Theory of Tropes in Anthropology.* Ed. James W. Fernandez. Stanford, CA: Stanford University Press, 1991. 121–58.

Ulmer, Gegory L. *Applied Grammatology: Post(e)-Pedagogy from Jacques Derrida to Joseph Beuys*. Baltimore: Johns Hopkins University Press, 1985.

————. "Textshop for Psychoanalysis: De-Programming Freshman Platonists." *College English* 49 (1987): 756–69.

Volosinov, V. N. *Marxism and the Philosophy of Language*. Trans. L. Matejka and I. R. Titunik. New York: Seminar, 1973.

Walzer, Michael. *Interpretation and Social Criticism*. Cambridge, MA: Harvard University Press, 1987.

Warnock, John. "The Writing Process." *Research in Composition and Rhetoric: A Bibliographical Sourcebook*. Eds. Michael G. Moran and Ronald F. Lunsford. Westport, CT: Greenwood, 1984. 3–26.

Wells, Susan. "Habermas, Communicative Competence, and the Teaching of Technical Discourse." *Theory in the Classroom*. Ed. Cary Nelson. Urbana: University of Illinois Press, 1986. 245–69.

West, Cornel. *The American Evasion of Philosophy: A Genealogy of Pragmatism*. Madison: University of Wisconsin Press, 1989.

Will, George. "The New Campus Hegemony: Every Academic Activity Must Reform Society." *The Philadelphia Inquirer*, 7 Sept. 1990, 27.

Williams, Raymond. *Writing in Society*. London: Verso, 1984.

Willis, Susan. *A Primer for Daily Life*. London: Routledge, 1991.

Winterowd, W. Ross. "From Brain to Ballpoint." *Composition/Rhetoric: A Synthesis*. Carbondale: Southern Illinois University Press, 1986. 27–39.

————. " 'Topics' and Levels in the Composing Process." *College English* 34 (1973): 701–09.

Zavarzadeh, Mas'ud, and Donald Morton. "Theory Pedagogy Politics: The Crisis of 'The Subject' in the Humanities." *Theory/Pedagogy/Politics: Texts for Change*. Ed. Donald Morton and Mas'ud Zavarzadeh. Urbana: University of Illinois Press, 1991. 1–32.

Index

About the Author

ALAN W. FRANCE is Assistant Professor of English and Director of Composition at West Chester University in Pennsylvania. He has published "Assigning Places: The Function of Introductory Composition as a Cultural Discourse," *College English* (October 1993).

ISBN 0-89789-403-0

EAN

9 780897 894036

9 0 0 0 0>